WHEN IS TRUE BELIEF KNOWLEDGE?

—————————————•ⅢⅢ•—————————————

PRINCETON MONOGRAPHS IN PHILOSOPHY

—————————— ·ꟼℳP· ——————————

The Princeton Monographs in Philosophy series offers short
historical and systematic studies on a wide variety
of philosophical topics.

Justice Is Conflict by Stuart Hampshire

Liberty Worth the Name: Locke on Free Agency by Gideon Yaffe

Self-Deception Unmasked by Alfred R. Mele

Public Goods, Private Goods by Raymond Geuss

Welfare and Rational Care by Stephen Darwall

A Defense of Hume on Miracles by Robert J. Fogelin

Kierkegaard's Concept of Despair by Michael Theunissen

Physicalism, or Something Near Enough by Jaegwon Kim

Philosophical Myths of the Fall by Stephen Mulhall

Fixing Frege by John P. Burgess

Kant and Skepticism by Michael N. Forster

Thinking of Others: On the Talent for Metaphor by Ted Cohen

The Apologetics of Evil: The Case of Iago by Richard Raatzsch

Social Conventions: From Language to Law by Andrei Marmor

Taking Wittgenstein at His Word: A Textual Study by Robert J. Fogelin

The Pathologies of Individual Freedom: Hegel's Social Theory
by Axel Honneth

Michael Oakeshott's Skepticism by Aryeh Botwinick

*Hegel on Self-Consciousness: Desire and Death in the Phenomenology of
Spirit* by Robert B. Pippin

Locke on Personal Identity: Consciousness and Concernment
by Galen Strawson

When Is True Belief Knowledge? by Richard Foley

WHEN IS TRUE
BELIEF KNOWLEDGE?

Richard Foley

PRINCETON UNIVERSITY PRESS

PRINCETON AND OXFORD

Copyright © 2012 by Princeton University Press

Requests for permission to reproduce material from this work
should be sent to Permissions, Princeton University Press

Published by Princeton University Press, 41 William Street,
Princeton, New Jersey 08540

In the United Kingdom: Princeton University Press, 6 Oxford
Street, Woodstock, Oxfordshire OX20 1TW

press.princeton.edu

Library of Congress Cataloging-in-Publication Data
Foley, Richard, 1947–
When is true belief knowledge? / Richard Foley.
p. cm. — (Princeton monographs in philosophy)
Includes bibliographical references (p.   ) and index.
ISBN 978-0-691-15472-5 (hardcover : alk. paper)
1. Knowledge, Theory of. 2. Belief and doubt. I. Title.
BD215.F587 2012
121—dc23   2012000421

British Library Cataloging-in-Publication Data is available

This book has been composed in Jason

Printed on acid-free paper. ∞

Printed in the United States of America

1 3 5 7 9 10 8 6 4 2

Contents

I

The Basic Idea

Chapter 1

An Observation

Someone glances at a clock that is not working and comes to believe it is quarter past seven. It in fact is quarter past seven. Her belief is true, but it isn't knowledge. Out of this classic example comes a classic philosophical question: what must be added to a true belief in order to make it into a plausible candidate for knowledge?

The answer is to be found in the observation that whenever someone has a true belief but does not know, there is important information she lacks. Seemingly a modest point, but it has the capacity to reorient the theory of knowledge.

For this observation to be philosophically useful, information needs to be understood independently of knowledge. The everyday notions of knowledge and information are intertwined, but every philosophical account has to start somewhere, helping itself to assumptions that can be revisited if they lead to difficulties. I begin by assuming that having information is a matter of having true beliefs.[1]

Substituting true belief for information, the core observation becomes that when someone has a true belief but does not know, there is some significant aspect of the situation about which she lacks true beliefs—something important that she doesn't grasp or doesn't quite "get." Knowledge is a matter of having adequate information, where the test of adequacy is negative. One must not lack important true beliefs. One knows that a red ball is on the mat in the hallway if one believes that this is so, the belief is true, and there is no important gap in one's information.

Information comes in various sizes and shapes, however. The red ball on the mat in the hallway has a precise circumference. It has a definite weight. It is made of rubber. The rubber is a certain shade of red. The mat likewise has its specific characteristics. So does the hallway. Its ceiling is of a certain height. Its walls are covered with black walnut paneling. There is a mahogany door leading outside. There are historical truths about the situation as well. The black walnut paneling was installed last year. The ball was bought two months ago at a Target store in Brooklyn. These historical truths are connected with yet others. The rubber making up the ball came from a tree grown on a rubber plantation in Kerala, India, which also grows tea. There is also negative information. The ball is not made of steel and is not larger than a standard basketball. There is not a bicycle in the hallway. Nor is there a truck or an oak tree. The hallway does not have a linoleum floor.

There is no end to the truths associated with there being a red ball on the mat in the hallway. They radiate out in all directions. Nor is this unusual. Every situation is lush, brimming over with truths.

The information we have is by comparison arid. No one, no matter how well informed, is in possession of all truths about a situation. If the number of such truths is not infinite, it is at least mind numbingly vast. Our grasps of situations are inevitably partial. Not all partial grasps are equal, however. Sometimes the information we lack is important, but sometimes not. If not, we know.

Whether a true belief counts as knowledge thus hinges on the importance of the information one has and lacks. This means that questions of knowledge cannot be separated from questions about human concerns and values. It also means that there is no privileged way of coming to know. Knowledge is a mutt. Proper pedigree is not required. What matters is that one not lack important nearby information.

This is getting ahead of the story, however. The best way to get a handle on this way of thinking about knowledge and to see how it reorients the theory of knowledge is to contrast it with received views.

Chapter 2

Post-Gettier Accounts of Knowledge

Before leaving her office, Joan always places her laptop on the corner of her desk. Unbeknownst to her, the laptop has just been stolen and is now sitting on the corner of a desk in the thief's apartment. Joan believes that her laptop is on the corner of a desk, and in fact it is, but she doesn't know this.

On Tuesday evening Mary went to sleep at 11 p.m. as is her habit, unaware that she had been given a sleeping potion that would cause her to sleep thirty-two hours instead of her usual eight. When she awakes in her heavily curtained and clockless bedroom on Thursday morning, she believes it is about 7 a.m., because this is the hour at which she regularly wakes. It is 7 a.m., but she nonetheless doesn't know this to be the case.

Jim has bought a ticket in a lottery of a million tickets. The winning ticket has been chosen but not yet announced. Jim believes that his ticket is not the winner and he is correct, but he lacks knowledge.

Examples such as these, which can be multiplied indefinitely, create an agenda for the theory of knowledge, that of identifying what has to be added to true belief in order to get knowledge. One tradition says that what is needed is something like an argument in defense of the belief, a justification to use the term of art. In an influential 1963 article, however, Edmund Gettier used a pair of examples to illustrate that justification on its own is not enough, and as a result the question became what has to be added to justified true belief in order to get knowledge?[1]

There has been no shortage of answers. Many have suggested that what is needed is a special kind of justification. The justification has to be nondefective in the sense that it must not justify any falsehoods,[2] or it has to be indefeasible in that it cannot be defeated by the addition of any truth.[3]

A rival tradition maintains that justification-based approaches are misdirected. Since we often are not in a position to defend what we know, something less explicitly intellectual than justification traditionally understood is required to understand knowledge, in particular, something about the processes and faculties that produce or sustain the belief.

Again, there has been no shortage of proposals. One popular idea is that for a true belief to count as knowledge, it must be reliably generated.[4] A second idea is that in close counterfactual situations, the subject's beliefs about the matter in question would track the truth.[5] A third is that the belief must be the product of properly functioning cognitive faculties.[6] There are also important variants of each of these ideas.[7]

All these proposals assume that what needs to be added to true belief in order to get knowledge is something related to true belief but distinct from it—nondefective justification, indefeasible justification, reliability, truth tracking in close counterfactual situations, proper functioning, or whatever. My suggestion, by contrast, is that whenever an individual S has a true belief P but does not know P, there is important information she lacks.

What has to be added to S's true belief P in order to get knowledge? More true beliefs. Especially more true beliefs in the neighborhood of P. In particular, there must not be important truths of which she is unaware, or worse, ones she positively disbelieves.

A merit of this view is that there is a straightforward way to test it. If S has a true belief P but does not know P, then according to the view it ought to be possible to identify a proposition Q such that (i) Q is an important truth and (ii) S does not believe Q.

Why does Joan not know that her laptop is on the corner of a desk, and Mary not know that it is 7 a.m., and Jim not know that his lottery ticket is not the winner, even though their beliefs are true? They lack key true beliefs about the situations in question. Joan isn't aware that her laptop has been stolen and that the desk on which it now sits is that of the thief; Mary isn't aware that she is just waking up from a drug-induced sleep; and Jim isn't aware which ticket has won the lottery.

This in brief is the idea I will be developing, but I want first to take a step back to look at the role of examples such as these in the theory of knowledge.

Chapter 3

Knowledge Stories

Contemporary theory of knowledge is driven by stories. The practice is to tell a tiny story, use it to elicit an intuition about whether the subject has or lacks knowledge, and then draw a moral for the theory of knowledge.

Some of the stories are stripped-down versions of familiar situations. Others depict unusual circumstances, such as my story about Mary and her drug-induced sleep. Still others are beyond unusual—for example, stories about brains in vats.

Sartre once remarked that in writing philosophy the aim is to discourage multiple interpretations, whereas in writing fiction the aim is precisely the opposite, to create texts that resist a single interpretation. Whether fiction or philosophy must have such aims is debatable, but the remark is instructive for the small fictions of contemporary epistemology. The stories are created in hopes of fixing upon some point or other about knowledge, but the stories are incomplete and hence open to different interpretations as well as to expansions that potentially blunt the intended point. The sparely told stories common in epistemology are especially susceptible. The fewer the details, the more room there is for interpretation and retelling.

Such stories can nonetheless be useful, but need to be treated warily. More on this later. For now the points to note are that contemporary theory of knowledge is driven by stories in which the subject has a true belief but seems to lack knowledge; the scenarios I sketch above (of Joan, Mary, and Jim) are themselves examples of such stories; these stories, mine included, make use of the common literary device of providing the audience with information that the subjects of the stories lack; and finally, the stories are told in a way to suggest that the missing information is important.

Consider a stock case from the literature. George is touring farm country and is charmed by the picturesque old barns he is seeing. He stops his car on the side of the road to spend a moment gazing at the latest barn he has happened across. Unbeknownst to him, the local tourist board has populated the region with highly realistic facades of old barns, and up until now he has been seeing these facades, not real barns. By chance, however, he has stopped in front one of the few genuine old barns remaining in the area. As he stares out of his car window, he believes that he is looking at an old barn and he is. Yet, there is a pull upon us, the audience listening to the story, which makes us reluctant to concede that his true belief rises to the level of knowledge.[1]

Why is this? Is it because the justification he has for his belief is defeasible, or because the processes that have caused him to have this belief are unreliable at this locale, or because his belief would not track the truth in close counterfactual situations? All these may well be the case, but the best explanation is the most obvious. He lacks important true beliefs about the situation. He is unaware that there are numerous, highly realistic barn facades in the area and unaware as well that on his tour up until now he has been seeing these facades instead of real barns.

The post-Gettier literature is filled with little stories about individuals who have true beliefs but seem to lack knowledge. All these stories can be understood in the same way. Each is an attempt to draw attention to some aspect of the situation about which the character of the story lacks true beliefs and to suggest that this aspect is in some way important. To the degree that we the audience are convinced that the missing information is in fact important, our intuition is that the character has a true belief but does not know.

I need now to take another step back and look at the role that intuitions such as these play in the theory of knowledge.

Chapter 4

Intuitions about Knowledge

Intuitions about whether someone knows something vary from person to person and occasion to occasion. Epistemologists react differently to this variation. Many ignore it. Some use it to question whether the ordinary concept of knowledge is coherent.[1] Still others try to impose uniformity by dismissing recalcitrant cases as ones in which the subject lacks "real knowledge"[2] or insisting on such high standards of knowledge that little can be known.[3]

My approach is not to be dismissive of intuitions about knowledge but at the same time to concede that they can be puzzling and even jumbled. Appealing to them is thus a messy and inconclusive business. They can be useful but only as starting points, not rigid constraints.

Besides, regarding knowledge intuitions as hard data to which theories have to conform makes for a timid epistemology. It invites questions of whose intuitions are supposed to matter. All those with the concept of knowledge? Philosophers? Some other group? It also suggests that the working procedure for epistemology ought to consist of surveying the intuitions of the relevant group, thereby collecting data as representative as possible. Few philosophers conduct such surveys, however, and with good reason. A philosophical account of knowledge ought to be made of loftier stuff.

What kind of "stuff"? It is more important to provide a framework that can be used to explain how and why intuitions arise than to conform to a set of favored intuitions, and more important still that the framework can be used to engage the various philosophical questions and puzzles that arise about knowledge, from why knowledge is valuable and what its relationship is with justified belief to whether it can be acquired by luck and why it is we are so often willing to admit that something we believe to be true is nonetheless not something we know. This in any event is my project.

There are limitations as to what can be expected of any such project, however, and not just because the intuitions are not uniform and the puzzles difficult. There are also distinct species of knowledge, which require special treatments.

There is knowledge of people, places, and things; one knows Mike Bloomberg, Greenwich Village, and various Internet sites. There is also knowledge of concepts, knowledge, for example, of what valid and sound arguments are and what an irrational number is. In addition, there is knowledge of subject areas; one knows American baseball and New York City politics. Knowledge how is yet something different—for example, knowing how to fix a faulty electrical switch or how to convert centigrade readings to Fahrenheit. There is knowledge of facts as well, some scientific (the boiling point of water is 212°F), others geographical (Accra is the capital of Ghana), still others historical (Thomas Jefferson was the third president of the United States), and many others personal (one is six feet tall).

Nor is knowledge always restricted to humans. Dogs are said to know that their owners are approaching and birds that a storm is due. Even body parts are sometimes said to know; the liver knows when to excrete bile. Knowledge is also attributed to machines; my laptop knows when to shut itself down to prevent overheating.

Some of these attributions are no doubt metaphorical. No matter. My focus is on knowledge of facts and specifically knowledge of facts by individual human beings as opposed to collective human knowledge.[4] Such knowledge may be linked with other kinds. It may even be the ground for some, but there are challenges enough in providing an account of it, because even within this category, there is striking variation, especially with respect to the amount of information required.

Often the presupposition is that broad and deep information is required for knowledge, but sometimes only scanty information seems necessary. A contestant on a quiz show is asked the date of the Battle of Marathon. She recalls from her high school world history course that it took place in 490 BCE, but does not remember that the Greeks won the battle or even that the adversaries were the Greeks and Persians. Still, it may seem as if she at least knows the date.[5]

Why such variation? Because in order to have knowledge, one must have adequate information, where the test of adequacy is that one not lack important surrounding truths. In some circumstances, however, most of the surrounding truths do not strike us as being especially critical in order for the subject to "get" the important aspects of what is going on. Hence, it may not seem to matter much whether she believes them. In other circumstances, however, a great many of the surrounding truths seem to matter. Intuitions about how much information is needed for knowledge thus vary from situation to situation. Moreover, the tiny knowledge stories common in epistemology can be told to exploit this malleability.

All stories are structured to elicit reactions—laughter, sympathy, outrage, or whatever— and there are standard techniques available to the storyteller for generating these reactions. The most basic is selectivity. Real situations are lush, whereas stories are selectively incomplete. The storyteller decides which of a potentially limitless set of details about characters and settings to omit and which to include, and what emphasis to put on those that are included. The ways in which these storytelling decisions are made pull the reactions of listeners in one direction or another.

It is no different with knowledge stories. Stories in which a character has a true belief can be told to make gaps in her information seem important, but they can also be told to diminish the significance of whatever gaps there are. Call the latter a "narrow telling."

There are, moreover, techniques for narrowing a story, the most obvious of which is to so dwell upon the importance of the belief itself being true that it reduces the importance of other aspects of the situation. This is what is going on the story about the quiz show, but the same technique can be used with other stories. The barn story, for example, can be retold to lower the significance of George's being unaware of the barn facades at nearby locations.

Imagine that the barn where he has stopped his car was the location of an especially important event of his childhood. It was his memory of this event that motivated him at great time and expense to return to the region and seek out this specific location. Since he has no interest in the other locations he has passed through or in the other barns he has apparently been seeing, he has paid scant attention to them. It is this particular location that was the sole purpose of his trip.

As the story has been retold, it may no longer seem quite as important that George is unaware that there are barn facades at other locales in the region. If so, we the audience may be more ready to concede that he knows he is looking at an old barn, indeed, the very barn he remembers from his childhood.[6]

Can a story ever be told so narrowly that all that matters is whether one has a true belief? At first glance, it may seem that the story of the quiz show is a case of this sort. On the other hand, because beliefs come and go in clusters, there are built-in limitations on just how meager one's surrounding information can be while having a true belief P, and hence limitations also on how meager one's information can be while knowing P.

The truth that the Battle of Marathon occurred in 490 BCE is conceptually intertwined with various other truths. Some are about location: Marathon is the name of a site in Greece; Greece is located on the Mediterranean Sea, and the Mediterranean Sea is a body of water on planet Earth. Others are about time: BCE stands for "before the common era"; the date 490 makes use of a dating system that has a year as its core unit of time; and a year is the period of time it takes Earth to make a complete revolution around its sun. Still others are about battles: a battle is a large-scale fight between armed forces; an armed force is equipped with weapons; and weapons have the capacity to inflict harms. To know that the Battle of Marathon occurred in 490 BCE, the quiz show contestant may not need be aware of all of these linked truths, but she does have to be aware of many. Otherwise, it would be doubtful whether she even understands, much less knows, the proposition that the Battle of Marathon occurred in 490 BCE.

In addition, the acquisition of beliefs, even very simple ones, typically depends on background information about the circumstances, and this too imposes constraints on how scanty one's information can be. An individual enters the hallway, sees a ball on the mat, and comes to believe that there is a red ball on the mat, but she does so in the context of having such situation-specific information as she is not wearing red tinted glasses, the lighting in the room does not make everything appear red, and she does not suffer from red-green color blindness. Without such information, she may not have come to believe that there is a red ball on the mat.[7]

There are thus constraints on how limited one's information can be while still knowing. Even so, the Marathon story and others like it pull intuitions in the direction of at least extremely narrow knowledge. They do so by focusing attention on a truth around which the story revolves and by making clear that what matters most in the circumstances at hand is that the character is aware of this key truth.[8]

The larger lesson here, however, is again one of caution. The knowledge stories common to epistemology are thinly described and the intuitions they elicit malleable and variable. So, a degree of skepticism is in order. Not necessarily a full-throated skepticism but at least a guardedness, which makes one wary about the intuitions of others and correspondingly humble about one's own, the combination of which has the advantage of keeping discussions of knowledge from deteriorating into contests about whose intuitions are right. Trading intuitions is often not very different from trading insults.

Having taken a detour to look at knowledge stories and the intuitions they elicit, it is time to return to the question of how best to think about the distinction between knowledge and true belief.

Chapter 5

Important Truths

To divide true beliefs that potentially rise to the level of knowledge from those that do not, theories of knowledge identify a dimension for making the division. Other conditions may also need to be satisfied, but this dimension does the initial work in qualifying a true belief as a plausible candidate for knowledge

According to justification-based theories, the relevant dimension is the strength of the person's evidence. According to reliability theories, it is the degree of reliability of the processes generating the belief. For tracking theories, it is how extensive the range of counterfactual situations is in which the person's belief would track the truth.

Whatever the proposed dimension, there is no nonarbitrary way of specifying a precise point along it at which a true belief becomes a credible candidate for knowledge. Proponents of justification-based theories may insist that for an individual to know *P*, it has to be more probable than not on her evidence, or if they are willing to concede there is little we know, they may contend that the probability has to be 1, but between these extremes, it is not possible to identify an exact probability greater than .5 and less than 1 as the tipping point. It is similarly not possible for reliabilists to designate a precise degree of reliability as the knowledge boundary. Likewise for tracking theories. Exactly how extensive must be the range of counterfactual situations in which the person's belief would track the truth? Extensive enough to make the belief into a serious candidate for knowledge.

I have been arguing that the relevant dimension is not evidence, reliability, or truth tracking but rather information about the situation in which P is true. On this view too, there is no way to specify a precise threshold. How much information must one have in order for a true belief to qualify as knowledge? Enough.

On the other hand, there is a negative test. When someone knows P, there aren't important truths she lacks. There are always gaps in one's information, but when one knows, the missing information isn't important.

If there is a dispute about whether someone knows something, this is not a test that will necessarily resolve it. Then again, it is not the job of a theory of knowledge to adjudicate hard cases. Its task, rather, is to explain how and why knowledge intuitions arise and in so doing address various questions and puzzles that arise about knowledge. Among the intuitions to be explained, however, are those about hard cases. A theory of knowledge ought to be able to shed light on what issues are at stake in hard cases and why intuitions about them are apt to vary.

Disputes over whether someone knows something arise in a variety of ways. If two spectators agree that an individual S believes P but disagree whether P is true, it won't be surprising if they have different views about whether she knows P. Likewise, if they agree that P is true but disagree whether she really believes it or disagree about what additional information she has, it again shouldn't be surprising if they reach different conclusions about whether she knows. But in addition, their disagreement[1] can be the result of different takes on whether a gap in her information is important, and often it is this that makes hard cases hard.

Disagreements over the importance of something are never easy to resolve, in part because there are different ways in which something can be important. Whenever issues of importance arise, it is always appropriate to ask, important in what respect? It is no different when the issue is the importance of missing information.

Knowledge is true belief plus adequate information. So, the kind of importance relevant to assessments of knowledge is importance with respect to the subject's having adequate information. If a truth strikes us as one that the subject needs to be aware of in order to have adequate information about the situation, then the truth is important in the relevant sense. Her not being aware of it would incline us to think she doesn't know.

What kinds of truths tend to strike us as being important in this sense? Whatever their other limitations, intuitions about knowledge stories are a resource for addressing this question. Collectively they constitute an inventory of sorts about the kinds of truths that observers think a subject needs to be aware of if she is to have knowledge.

An especially common type of knowledge story involves a subject who has a true belief but is unaware of some shortcoming that afflicts either her or her belief. Some of the stories, for example, narrate a scenario in which S has evidence for her true belief P but is unaware of something that would undermine this evidence. Although her belief P is true, in many situations this kind of gap in her information would cause problems of accuracy. Hence, the missing information is apt to strike us as important, that is, as something S should be aware of if she is to have an adequate grasp of her situation.

Or consider stories in which S doesn't realize that the methods or faculties that have led her to believe P are unreliable in the situation in question. Even if the story makes clear that her belief P is true, this again can seem to be an important gap in her information, since in similar circumstances relying on such methods or faculties would lead to error.

In analogous ways, S's being unaware of other kinds of intellectual shortcomings can strike onlookers as potentially important. Although there is a variety of such shortcomings, it can be tempting to fasten upon stories involving a particular kind of shortcoming and to try to build an entire theory of knowledge around them. Stories in which S has a true belief P but is unaware of the untrustworthiness of the faculties or methods producing the belief motivate reliability or truth-tracking theories. Stories in which S is unaware of truths that constitute key evidence for P make justification-based approaches seem natural, whereas stories in which S is unaware of relevant truths that are widely available to others in her community encourage theories with a social dimension.

Each of these theories has undeniable appeal, because each captures a large class of cases in which the subject seems to lack knowledge despite having a true belief. They also share a limitation, however. Each seizes upon a specific intellectual drawback and tries to make it into the defining characteristic of knowledge, taking precedence over all the others.

My approach, by contrast, is ecumenical. There are

any number of intellectual shortcomings that can afflict S or her belief such that if she is unaware of them, she will lack knowledge. None has a privileged status.

Proponents of other approaches, of course, maintain that it is the shortcoming itself—the unreliability of the process causing the belief or the defectiveness of the justification or whatever—rather than S's lack of awareness of it that is the problem. One way of pressing this point is to imagine that S becomes aware of the deficiency but nonetheless continues to believe P. Wouldn't we still be inclined to say she lacks knowledge?

For example, retell the barn story so that George becomes aware that the region in which he is driving his car is populated with barn facades so realistic that from the road it is impossible to distinguish them from genuine barns. Yet as he sits in his car and stares out his window, he believes he is looking at a real barn. Since he has happened to stop in front of one of the few genuine barns remaining in the region, his belief is correct, but most listeners will be no more inclined than in the original case to think that he knows.

Agreed, but this is now a new story, and in this new story we are led once again to think George lacks important information. It's just different information from the original story. In the original he lacked information about the facades. As the story has been retold, the important information he lacks is how the thing he sees from his car window looks close up and from the rear and sides.

Why do we think that it is important for him to have such information? There are various possible rationales. Here is one: in the retold story George is aware that there are highly realistic barn facades in the region, and this defeats the presumptive credibility of his observa-

tions from the car window; as a result, if he is to be justified in believing he is looking at a barn, he needs to get
out of the car and observe the thing close-up and from all
sides, whereas in the original story it was reasonable for
him to trust his observations from his car's window. Here
is another: getting out of the car and observing the barn-
like thing close-up is the only way in these circumstances
for him to have a reliably produced belief about whether
what he is seeing is in fact a barn. In other words, some
of the rationales for thinking the missing information is
important track the explanations that justification theorists, reliability theorists, or proponents of other approaches would give for why George lacks knowledge.
These approaches provide a directory to the sorts of gaps
that are apt to strike observers as important.

We needn't choose among these approaches, however.
We can be ecumenical. Any and all—reliability accounts,
tracking accounts, proper function accounts, justification-
based accounts, etc.—can be helpful in identifying the
kinds of truths we think the subject must be aware of if
she is to have adequate information.

Let's pursue the point here a bit further, since it might
be objected that although this reply works well enough
for the revised barn story in which George becomes aware
that there are facades in the region, it merely pushes the
issue back a level. To illustrate, imagine a case in which a
subject S is aware of as many surrounding truths about
the situation as one wishes. A reliabilist will still maintain
that if S's true belief P was not reliably produced, it is not
an instance of knowledge. In particular, it doesn't matter
if she herself is aware that her belief P is not the product
of a reliable process. Ditto for justification theorists,
tracking theorists, proper function theorists, and others.

They too will claim that no matter how many surrounding truths S acquires, including truths to the effect that her justification is defective or her belief wouldn't track the truth or was not the product of properly functioning faculties or whatever, she does not have knowledge if her belief P has the shortcoming in question.

Not so fast, however. It may not be as easy as one imagines for there to be circumstances in which S believes as many surrounding truths as possible and yet still has the shortcoming in question. We need to fill in some of the details of the case as a way of testing whether this really is possible. In addition, even if in the end we decide that such a case is possible, once we have fully digested in some detail what it would look like, it may no longer seem so obvious that S lacks knowledge. I will be describing just such a case in the next chapter and using it to illustrate differences between the view that knowledge is to be understood in terms of adequate information and other views.

Before doing so, however, there is another issue to be surfaced, which is that practical as well as intellectual considerations can influence assessments about whether a truth is important enough that S must be aware it if she is to have knowledge.

One of the core tenets of pragmatist epistemology is that there is no purely intellectual measure for how important a piece of information is. Information about the atomic numbers of various chemical elements is generally regarded as more important than information about how many grains of salt there are in a shaker of salt, but not because the former is intrinsically more significant and not solely for intellectual reasons either. Its importance derives rather from complex links with our lives in all their detail, and in particular, with the full range of human concerns and values.

Intuitions about whether someone has enough information for knowledge are likewise influenced by such links. Consider a foreman who works in a factory that makes highly noxious chemicals and who is responsible for the air purification equipment at the factory. He is aware that the equipment is exceedingly well engineered and aware also there has never been a problem with it during the two years it has been in operation. His job nonetheless requires him to inspect the equipment daily, which he does on his morning rounds. There is a warning light on the equipment that is green when the equipment is working properly and red when it is not purifying the air. The foreman is unaware that the warning mechanism has just shorted so that even if there were a problem with the equipment, the green light would remain on. He could have disconnected the purifier elements to check whether the warning light is functioning properly, but he does not. He looks at the light, sees that it is green, and believes that the equipment is purifying the air just as it always has for the past two years. Moreover, he is correct. The equipment is working perfectly.

Some listeners in hearing this story will be reluctant to grant that the foreman knows that the equipment is purifying the air, despite the fact that the equipment is in fact doing so and he has lots of evidence to this effect. Why? Because the story has been told to make the gap in the foreman's information about the warning light seem important. After all, he is responsible for the equipment, and the stakes of his being mistaken are potentially very high.

Consider now another story that is in most ways analogous, only the stakes are not nearly so high. The same foreman before going to work at the factory each day uses an electric toaster to toast a piece of bread. The toaster has a small light that is green if the toaster is working properly and red if the coils are not heating sufficiently to toast bread. The make of his toaster has an extremely high reliability rating, and the foreman has never had a problem with it in the two years he has owned it. Unbeknownst to him, however, the warning mechanism in the toaster has just shorted in such a way that the light would be green even if the heating coils were not working. As he begins to prepare his breakfast, he could have gone to the trouble of disconnecting the coils to test whether the warning light is functioning properly, but he does not. He pushes the handle of the toaster down, the green light illuminates, and he starts to prepare his coffee, believing that his bread is toasting as usual, and indeed it is. The heating coils are toasting the bread just as they have day in and day out for the past two years.

Those who are reluctant to grant that in the first story the foreman knows may be more willing to do so here. If so, why? Because the story has been told to make clear that the foreman has lots of evidence about the reliability of the toaster and to make clear as well that the stakes of his being wrong are minor. As a result, the gap in his information may not seem all that significant.[2]

In *Knowledge and Practical Interests*, Jason Stanley presents an assortment of examples to illustrate that standards of knowledge tend to become more demanding as the practical stakes go up.[3] Not everyone has been persuaded by his examples but many have, and the view that knowledge is best thought of in terms of adequate information helps explain why.

Whenever S believes P and P is true, there are inevitably gaps in her information about the situation. The question is whether the gaps are important enough to prevent her from having enough information to know. The knowledge stories of contemporary epistemology help answer this question by creating an inventory of truths which, when missing, strike many observers as being important in this sense. A good number of the stories are ones in which the subject is unaware of something that has the potential to have adverse effects on her performance as an intellectual being, but the stories now being considered are ones that draw attention to her being unaware of something that has the potential to have adverse effects on her performance as an agent. If a gap in her information could result in her producing (or not preventing) harm, there is a presumption that the gap is important. Indeed, all else being equal, the greater the potential for harm, the stronger the presumption.

All else is not always equal, however. Closeness also counts. When an individual S believes that there is a red ball on the mat in the hallway, there is no end to the truths associated with the situation, but some, even if otherwise consequential, seem too remote to be important when appraising whether she has enough information to know.[4]

The red ball on the mat in the hallway was purchased at a Target store two months ago; several years ago an identical ball (size, color, brand) was shoplifted from the same Target store; the shoplifter, whose father was a candidate for mayor at the time, was caught and prosecuted;

and the father lost the election as a result of the negative publicity, which in turn led to major changes in city policies. These are consequential truths, but we are unlikely to regard S's ignorance of them as preventing her from having enough information to know there is a red ball on the mat in the hallway, since as far as we can tell, they are not involved in any significant way either with her believing that there is a red ball on the mat or with this belief's being true.

Some propositions are so closely connected with P that it is neither possible for P to be true without their also being true nor possible for S to believe P without also believing them. At the other extreme are truths so distant conceptually, spatially, temporally, or causally that they play no discernible role in her believing P or in P's being true. Between these two extremes are truths that play some role, greater or less, either in P's being true or in S's believing P. The more direct and essential we regard these roles as being, then all else being equal, the more we will be inclined to regard S's lack of awareness of them as potentially interfering with her having adequate enough information for knowledge.

Once again, however, all else is not always equal. As discussed earlier, in circumstances of narrow knowledge, little seems to matter beyond the truth of the belief itself. Being aware of additional truths thus tends to strike us as unnecessary, however close or distant they may be. The quiz show contestant who is asked the date of the Battle of Marathon and replies straight away "490 BCE" may not be aware of neighboring truths about the battle, and yet we still may be inclined to grant that she at least knows the date.[5]

Knowledge stories push and pull intuitions about, but

the pushes and pulls do not affect everyone in the same way—hence, disputes about knowledge arise. There is, however, a standard dynamic at play in these disputes. For those who think that S has a true belief P but does not know, it will seem that there are truths she lacks that are important for her to have if she is to have adequate information about the situation in question, where the standards of what counts as adequate can be affected by the practical stakes of her being right or wrong. At the extreme are those with skeptical leanings who will be quick to regard almost any gap in her information as important. By contrast, for those who think that she does know, it will seem that the truths she lacks are not important enough to prevent her from having adequate information about P. Indeed, it may even seem that the circumstances are such that little beyond the truth of P itself matters. Its truth swamps everything else.

Some may wish for a theory of knowledge that takes definitive stands on such disputes, but my aim is neither to adjudicate hard cases nor to offer a theory of importance. It is rather to illustrate that it is our takes on the importance of missing information, however formed, that generate intuitions about knowledge stories, and to illustrate also that intuitions about such stories can conflict, and when they do, the complexity and variety of factors affecting them can make it difficult to resolve the disputes.

This is a less confrontational approach than some might desire, but it has the advantage of not pretending that intuitions about knowledge are clean data to which theories must be adequate. Intuitions about knowledge just are varied and they just are messy. The task for a theory of knowledge is not to clean up the mess but to explain it.[6]

This is not to say that there aren't cases where the adequate information view clearly points in a different direction from other approaches, but it is in extreme cases where these differences are most evident. I now turn to such a case.

Chapter 6

Maximally Accurate and Comprehensive Beliefs

To know one must not lack important information. This test may not always resolve disputes over whether someone knows something, but it does suggest that as one's grasp of a situation becomes more and more complete, it ought to become more and more difficult to deny that one has knowledge.

Merely accumulating truths is not enough, however. One can acquire numerous truths about a situation and still not be in a position to know if the truths are unimportant. Moreover, how truths are connected is itself information, indeed, often crucial information.

Two-thirds of the way through a mystery novel, it may be obvious to readers that the detective has a true belief that the victim's childhood friend is the guilty party and obvious as well that the detective has discovered all the essential clues—the weapon, the jimmied lock, the empty safe, and so on. Nonetheless, if the detective is unable to piece together these clues into an accurate picture of when, how, and why the crime was committed, readers are likely to think that the detective does not yet have enough information to know that the childhood friend is the guilty party. The significant gap in his information is how the bits of information in his possession fit together.[1]

So, sheer quantity of information is not what makes it difficult to deny someone has knowledge. The point, rather, is that as someone comes to have an increasingly comprehensive grasp of a situation, where this involves not only having the important pieces of information but also seeing how they are linked, it should become increasingly difficult to maintain that she doesn't know.

Let's push this thought to its limit. Imagine Sally's beliefs are as accurate and comprehensive as it is humanly possible for them to be. She has true beliefs about the basic laws of the universe, and in terms of these she can explain what has happened, is happening, and will happen. She can explain the origin of the universe, the origin of the earth, the origin of life on earth, the mechanisms by which cells age, and the year in which the sun will die. She even has a complete and accurate explanation of how it is that she came to have all this information.

Consider a truth $Pcells$ about the aging mechanisms in cells. Sally believes $Pcells$, and because her beliefs about these mechanisms are maximally accurate and comprehensive, there are few gaps of any sort in her information, much less important ones. Thus, she knows $Pcells$.

According to many theories, however, a true belief can be an instance of knowledge only if it has a proper ancestry, with there being competing views about what the required lineage is. Some maintain that the belief must be caused in an appropriate way by the facts that make it true; others hold that it must be the product of cognitive processes that are generally reliable about matters of the kind in question; still others say that it must be the product of cognitive faculties functioning as they were designed to function.

It is consistent with the Sally story as told that her beliefs about how cells age were not caused by the facts that make them true and were not the products of reliable processes or properly functioning cognitive faculties. Rather, it may have been some combination of curious processes and unlikely events that led to her having these beliefs. But Sally is fully aware that however strange and unlikely this history may be, in her case it led to her having maximally accurate and comprehensive beliefs.

Ancestral accounts are nevertheless committed to denying that she knows Pcells or for that matter much of anything else. Indeed, on the assumption that the rest of us often have a good many true beliefs with the required ancestry, these accounts imply that we know more about the world than Sally does. By contrast, the adequate information view implies that Sally has far greater knowledge than the rest of us even if the way she acquired it is unusual. But if so, no special pedigree is needed for knowledge. Knowledge can be a mutt. One has to have adequate information, but there is no privileged way of getting it.

Intuitions can and do vary, however, especially about stories far removed from the ordinary. So, the aim here is not so much to set up a battle of intuitions but rather to illustrate differences between approaches. According to reliability theories, it does not matter that Sally has as accurate and comprehensive grasp of Pcells as it is possible for a human to have. What matters is whether her beliefs about Pcells were reliably produced. By contrast, on the adequate information approach, having beliefs that are reliably produced is a frequent accompaniment of knowledge but not a strict prerequisite. Since there are few if any gaps, much less important ones, in Sally's information about *P*cells, she knows.

This story can be also used to highlight differences with other accounts of knowledge. Consider tracking theories. It is possible for Sally's beliefs to be maximally accurate and comprehensive and yet not track the truth in close counterfactual situations. But then, according to tracking accounts, she does not have knowledge, whereas on the adequate information approach, this would again seem implausible. She has maximally accurate and comprehensive beliefs about the origin of the universe, how life came into existence on earth, and the mechanisms by which cells age, and if unusual circumstances led her to have these beliefs, she also has maximally accurate and comprehensive beliefs about these circumstances. In particular, if her beliefs would not track the truth in close counterfactual situations, she is fully aware of this and has true beliefs about why they would not do so. She is aware, in effect, of the fragility of her information. Fragility, however, is not necessarily incompatible with knowledge. Think by analogy of powerfully precise measuring instruments whose workings are so delicate that if the operating conditions were altered so that there were even minor vibrations present, their readings would no longer be accurate, but as long as there are no such vibrations, these counterfactual inaccuracies are beside the point. So it may be with Sally's beliefs.[2]

What about justification-based theories of knowledge? Since Sally can fully explain the origin of the universe, the origin of the earth, and the mechanisms by which cells age, it might seem that her beliefs about these matters must be justified. On the other hand, some of the most familiar accounts of justified belief imply that one's beliefs are justified only if they are structured in a specific way, but it's not a foregone conclusion that Sally's beliefs have the required structure.

Consider classical foundationalist accounts, which imply that beliefs are justified only if they can be adequately defended in terms of self-justifying beliefs, where the only beliefs that are self-justifying are ones about simple necessary truths and current psychological states. There is nothing in the story about Sally that guarantees that her beliefs about the origin of the universe, how life came into existence on earth, and the mechanisms by which cells age can be adequately defended in terms of such beliefs. Nor is there anything that prevents Sally herself from being fully aware that her beliefs cannot be so defended despite being maximally accurate and comprehensive.

Or consider accounts that require justified beliefs to be coherent, where coherence is a matter of the logical and probabilistic relations among the beliefs, and then go on to use intellectual virtues such as simplicity and conservatism to distinguish among equally coherent but competing sets of beliefs. There again are no assurances that Sally's beliefs meet these requirements. A set of beliefs that is maximally accurate and comprehensive is not necessarily the most coherent, simple, and conservative. Moreover, once again, Sally may realize all this. She can be aware that her beliefs, although maximally accurate and comprehensive, do not satisfy the requirements of coherence accounts of justified beliefs.

The apparent lesson is that just as a special ancestry is not required for true beliefs to count as knowledge, nei-

ther is a special structure. I say "apparent" not only because intuitions about cases as extraordinary as this have
to be treated with a grain of salt, but also because every
story is incomplete. The story about Sally is no exception,
and it might turn out that the details cannot be filled in
without implying that her beliefs have other merits—in
particular, merits related to ancestry or structure.

Might it be possible to argue, for example, that Sally's
beliefs couldn't possibly be maximally accurate and comprehensive unless they were reliably generated? This
would not be a simple argument to make, however, at
least not if the reliability in question is supposed to be
the kind that makes a true belief into a plausible candidate for knowledge. Reliability theorists go out of their
way to point out that a process that in fact produces only
true beliefs is not thereby necessarily reliable in the sense
they have in mind.[3] So, it is not enough merely to observe that the processes generating Sally's beliefs have
yielded only true beliefs.

On the other hand, there may be ways of arguing for a
more modest conclusion, in particular, that the Sally story
cannot be filled in without assuming an orderly universe
that she has interacted with in lawlike ways, which in turn
imply that her beliefs have to be the products of processes
that meet at least minimal standards of reliability. But if
so, so be it. Indeed, so much the better, since this makes it
all the easier to accept that Sally has knowledge. Not only
does she have views about Pcells that are as comprehensive and accurate as is humanly possible, in addition her
views, although arrived in a highly unusual manner, have
to be the products of lawlike interactions that meet minimum conditions of reliability.

An argument of this sort, however, would not affect

the key point for purposes here, since the simplest and best explanation of why Sally knows is not that her beliefs are products of processes that are reliable in this minimal sense. All sorts of true beliefs meet this condition without being plausible candidates of knowledge. The explanation, rather, is that her beliefs are maximally accurate and comprehensive, and hence she lacks no important information. What such an argument, if successful, does reveal is a constraint on just how unreliable a set of processes can be and yet still produce maximally accurate and comprehensive beliefs.

Just as it may be possible to argue that maximally accurate and comprehensive beliefs inevitably satisfy minimal standards of reliability, so too it may be possible to argue that they inevitably meet minimal standards of justification. Donald Davidson maintained that it is not possible to attribute beliefs to others, much less knowledge, without the attributed states being largely coherent.[4] Even if Davidson overstates the point and the nature of belief doesn't itself produce such strong constraints on the structure of one's beliefs, the world may do so, or more cautiously may do so to the degree that the beliefs are accurate and comprehensive. One line of argument, for example, is that it is not possible for beliefs to be maximally accurate and comprehensive without reflecting whatever orderly structure the world has, and this orderliness in turn ensures that the beliefs meet minimal standards of coherence. Another line of argument, more foundationalist in spirit, is that maximally accurate and comprehensive beliefs cannot help but be derived in part from experiences of the world, since without such an experiential base, they could not have the content they need to have in order to be accurate and comprehensive.[5]

Once again, if such arguments can be made, they make it all the easier to accept that Sally has knowledge. Her beliefs may not be tethered to experience in quite the way that foundationalists typically insist and may not be coherent in quite the way that coherentists prefer, but they do have to be at least minimally coherent and tethered to experience. Thus at least in these respects, Sally begins to look at least a little more like an ordinary human knower.

Suppose, however, we assume the worst. Assume that all such arguments fail, and hence it is in principle possible for Sally's beliefs to be maximally accurate and comprehensive and yet not be even minimally coherent or minimally tied to experience or the products of even minimally reliable processes. What then? Might not we then be more reluctant to grant that Sally knows? Maybe, but even if this is so, why put much faith in this intuition, given that the situation being imagined is so far removed from our everyday attributions of knowledge and given also that her beliefs are as accurate and comprehensive as it is possible for human beliefs to be?

On the other hand, a dismissive response of this sort can all too easily be returned in kind, the rejoinder being, why put much faith in the intuition that she does know, given that the situation is so far removed from the ordinary and given that her beliefs don't meet minimal standards of coherence, reliability, or connectedness with experience? The real challenge, once again, is to avoid being forced into a position where we are simply trading intuitions.

So, let's agree to keep open the possibility that even if Sally's beliefs are as accurate and comprehensive as it is possible for human beliefs to have, something nonetheless might interfere with her knowing. As a first step toward seeing how the adequate information view might accommodate this possibility, I will now turn to an extreme story at the opposite end of the spectrum from the Sally story, one involving not an abundance of information but rather a scarcity.

Chapter 7

The Beetle in the Box

An individual S comes into room and sees a small, sealed box on the table. She looks at the outside of the box from all angles but cannot see into it. There is nothing unusual about its weight. Nor does it make a special sound when shaken. Relative to what she is able to observe, there might be nothing at all inside, or there might be a coin wrapped in cloth so as to make no noise, or perhaps a marble or a key. S, however, believes that there is a beetle in the box, and she is correct. There is in fact a beetle inside, but she does not know this to be the case.[1]

People know many things without having observed their truth firsthand. So, the reason that S here lacks knowledge isn't just that she has not been able to determine by inspection that there is a beetle inside. The problem is that in addition, as far as we can tell, she has no other information about how a beetle might have come to be inside the box.

Let H be the full history of this box and this beetle and how the beetle came to be inside in the box. If we were to stipulate that like Sally of the previous chapter, S has completely accurate and comprehensive beliefs about H, it would be plausible to say that she knows it contains a beetle even though she cannot see inside.

Suppose, on the other hand, that there is no rich history. The world is such that the beetle has always been in the box. This is just the way the world is. There is this box, and it has a beetle inside it.

Is this really possible? Ordinary boxes and ordinary beetles come into existence via specific histories. It is thus hard to conceive, that is, fully and completely conceive, how it could be that this box and beetle do not likewise have such histories. Whatever material the box is made of, must not it have come from somewhere? If the material is wood, the wood came from a specific tree that had a parent tree which itself had a parent tree, and at some point wood from the offspring tree was made into the box. Similarly with the beetle. If it is like other beetles, it came from parent beetles, which themselves had their own histories. Moreover, there is a history about how beetles in general came into existence.

Let's agree to stretch the limits of intelligibility and simply stipulate that there is no or at least very little meaningful history to be told about this beetle and this box. They didn't come into existence in the way that other boxes and beetles do. Since the beginning of time, there has been this box with a beetle inside. The history of the box and beetle is thus unconnected with the histories of how other things in the universe, including other beetles and other boxes, came into existence.

Suppose, finally, S believes all this to be the case. What then? Although she has a true belief that there is a beetle in the box, it still seems that she does not know this. And yet, what are the important truths she lacks? The view of knowledge I have been developing implies that if S here doesn't have knowledge, there are important truths she is lacking. Well, what are they?

Even in the case of this unusual box, there are ways of testing whether there is a beetle inside. An fMRI scan of the box would display a beetle-shaped image. A device that is able to detect and analyze DNA through the box would register beetle DNA. If one pried open the box, one would see a beetle. If such tests have been conducted but S is unaware of them, this can be used to explain why she lacks knowledge.

But suppose we now push the story a step further and stipulate that no such test has ever been conducted and none ever will be. Imagine if you wish that the box is sacred, tests on it are prohibited, and this prohibition is rigidly enforced. The religious mandate is that one should believe that the box has a beetle in it without having to resort to tests. To ensure this, the box is protected by sophisticated security systems that prevent observational access as well as any tests.

Even in a world where no tests are performed, there are counterfactual truths about what would happen were such tests to be conducted. Suppose, however, that S believes these truths. After all, if she believes that there is a beetle in the box and has enough background information, she can infer them. She believes that if an fMRI scan were taken of the box, it would display a beetle-shaped image; she likewise believes if a DNA-analyzing device were used on the box, it would register beetle DNA; she believes that if she were allowed to pry the box open, she would see a beetle; and so on for other counterfactual truths of this sort.

In sum, S believes that there is a beetle in the box; her

belief is true; she is aware of all the various counterfactual truths about what would happen were the box to be tested; and yet it still seems that she does not know that there is a beetle inside. The intuition here is that for all she knows, there could be a coin or a marble or nothing at all inside. If she had believed that there is a coin instead of a beetle inside, she would have inferred that were the appropriate coin detection tests to be employed on the box, they would confirm the presence of the coin. These inferences would have been false, since there isn't in fact a coin in the box. By contrast, all the beliefs she has inferred from her belief that there is a beetle in the box are true.

In thinking about this story, there are two points to keep in mind. The first is the familiar one that intuitions about knowledge are to be treated with caution. They vary from person to person and occasion to occasion, and moreover the stories that are used to elicit them can be told so as to push and pull them in one direction or another. They are not clean data to which theories of knowledge must be adequate, especially not when they are about situations as bizarre as this one. So, one response to the story is "bizarre world, bizarre knowledge." If S has all the important information there is to be had, she has knowledge.

Be this as it may, when the imagined circumstances are so far removed from those we are used to encountering, humility is in order. It's presumptuous to think there is only one acceptable stance to take toward such a case. So, in this ecumenical spirit, let's accede to the intuition that S here lacks knowledge. What then?

Then a second point comes into play, namely, it is important to distinguish the theory that knowledge is a matter of having adequate information from the standard way of testing whether someone has adequate information. For the theory is well positioned to explain why S does not know that there is a beetle in the box; she does not have enough information. What is peculiar about the case is that ordinarily when S has a true belief P but doesn't know, there are important available truths she lacks. In this case, however, she has all the important information there is to be had about P. There are no significant truths about the situation of which she is unaware. It is the world that is lacking, not S. The world is informationally impoverished with respect to the proposition that there is a beetle in the box. Indeed, so impoverished that the proposition is unknowable, whether by S or anyone else.

The story thus supports the basic insight of the theory (S doesn't know that there is a beetle in the box because she does not have adequate information) but also illustrates that the standard test for adequate information (there is no important truth she lacks) has restricted applicability. The test cannot be used when the imagined world is so informationally deprived with respect to P that P is not capable of being known. In a situation of this sort, knowledge is blocked.[2]

Chapter 8

Knowledge Blocks

Fanciful stories about circumstances far removed from those in which we typically make ascriptions of knowledge have to be handled with care. The stories themselves are underdescribed, and the intuitions they elicit are various and malleable. Such stories can nonetheless be instructive, as the beetle in the box illustrates. In any remotely normal situation, when S has a true belief P but does not know P, there are important truths she lacks, but in the beetle case there are no such truths and yet she seems not to have knowledge. Why? Because there is so little significant information to be had about the box that it is not possible for anyone to have adequate enough information to know that there is a beetle inside.[1]

Consider a modification of the story that makes it, if possible, even stranger. The new story begins the same as the original—there is beetle inside a sealed box; S looks at the outside of the box but cannot see into it; there is nothing distinctive about its weight; it makes no special sound when shaken; no one else has looked inside it; no tests have been performed on it; none ever will be—but in this version the beetle crawls out of the box for a few seconds once every million years and then crawls back in for the next million years. The last such appearance was five hundred thousand years ago, prior to the arrival of modern humans, and the next appearance will be five hundred thousand years hence, when who knows whether humans will be around to witness the event.[2]

Suppose, moreover, S believes all this; that is, she believes not only that there is a beetle in the box but also that the beetle momentarily appears outside of the box once every million years, with the last such appearance being five hundred thousand years ago. She thus has a bit more information than in the original version of the story. Nevertheless, the intuition is still likely to be that she is not in a position to know that there is a beetle in the box, and the explanation is the same. There is too little information available for anyone to know. Knowledge is still blocked.

Suppose the beetle comes out every ten thousand years instead of every million years. Does this make a difference? What about every thousand years or every one hundred or even every ten? As one retells the story to shrink the intervals between the beetle's appearances, the information potentially available to S and others at some point begins to look more like ordinary situations where one can know something without having witnessed it firsthand.

Without having looked inside her friend's suitcase, S can know that it contains a pair of binoculars if she is aware that her friend is on her way to Cape May, her friend is an avid bird-watcher, Cape May is a well-known bird-watching locale, the spring bird migrations have just begun, her friend had talked just the night before about which binoculars to take with her, a pair of binoculars was laid out on the bed along with the clothes she was taking, her friend is a careful packer, and so forth.

Similarly, if the appearances of the beetle become frequent enough, there will eventually be enough information potentially available that knowledge will no longer be blocked. Whether S knows there is a beetle in the box will then depend, as usual, on whether she possesses enough of this information or whether there are instead important gaps in her information.

Are there other ways in which knowledge can be blocked? Perhaps. It may be possible to dream up other strange situations in which we feel unease about granting that the subject knows even if there is no significant gap in her information. Situations in which there is something bizarre going on with one of the core components of knowledge (belief, truth, surrounding truths) are especially likely to make us uneasy.

On the other hand, there are always alternatives to introducing knowledge blocks. One is simply to live with the unease and insist that the subject does have knowledge despite there being an initial pull in the opposite direction. If the situation is bizarre enough, this need not be even much of a stretch. In addition, because knowledge stories are thinly described, it is always appropriate to consider what they look like when some of the details are filled in, because once details are added, our reactions to the stories may well be different.

Recall the story of Sally whose beliefs are maximally accurate and comprehensive. If knowledge is a matter of having adequate information, it would seem that she has all sorts of knowledge that ordinary humans lack. Yet, it is possible to imagine circumstances in which her beliefs, albeit maximally accurate and comprehensive, are so strangely acquired we may feel some reluctance to grant she knows. As discussed in chapter 6, however, when we consider these circumstances in more detail, it may emerge that her beliefs, being maximally accurate and comprehensive, must also have other merits, such as being at least minimally coherent or minimally tied to experience or produced by minimally reliable processes. If so, this may reassure us about her knowing. Her beliefs may not be coherent or tethered to experience or reliably produced in quite the ways that coherentists, foundationalists, and reliabilists favor, but they are at least minimally coherent, minimally tethered to experience and produced by minimally reliably processes. Moreover, they are as accurate and comprehensive as possible.

Then again, assume a worst-case scenario for the adequate information view. Assume that all such arguments fail, and hence it is possible for Sally's beliefs to be maximally accurate and comprehensive and yet not meet even minimal standards of reasonability, reliability, and the like. Assume also that some observers will have an intuition that under these conditions Sally does not have knowledge. It is at this point in a spirit of ecumenicism that blocking conditions can be introduced. They are a concession to the reality that intuitions about extreme cases are tenuous and apt to be diverse. Thus, the fallback position: insofar as there is a pull against knowledge despite the fact that Sally has a true belief P and lacks no important information about P, it is because something is interfering with the normal requirements of knowledge. In particular, it may be that some minimal standard is not being met. In the beetle case, it was minimal standards of information. Here in this Sally case, it may be minimal standards of coherence, reliability, or connectedness to experience.

This might be regarded as a retreat from the view that knowledge is a matter of having adequate information if there were some compelling, higher-level theory of blocking conditions, but there is not, only after-the-fact invocations of them as our imaginations soar and we concoct ever more extraordinary stories in which something is affecting one of the core conditions of knowledge in such extreme ways that intuitions about these cases are likely to vary.

In any event, however intriguing these cases at the borderlines of imagination may be, it is important to remember that they are at the borderlines. As such, they don't affect the basic insight of the adequate information view, which is that in any remotely normal situation, when S has a true belief P but lacks knowledge, there are important truths she lacks.[3]

Chapter 9

The Theory of Knowledge and Theory of Justified Belief

S knows *P* if her belief *P* is true and she has adequate information, but she and her belief will usually have various other merits as well. In most cases, her cognitive faculties will have functioned properly, she will have used reliable methods, she will have been appropriately careful in gathering and deliberating about the evidence, and so on.

Such merits are frequent accompaniments of knowledge but not prerequisites. If *S* has a true belief *P* and there is no important gap in her information, then except perhaps in a few highly unusual situations where knowledge may be blocked, she knows *P*. Nothing more is necessary to explain why she knows. Not even justification.

In his 1963 article, "Is Justified True Belief Knowledge?" Edmund Gettier argued that justification when added to true belief is not sufficient for knowledge, but he simply assumed that it is necessary.[1] He was not alone. This has been a common presupposition, but one that has had unfortunate consequences for both the theory of knowledge and the theory of justified belief—consequences that became conspicuous in the aftermath of Gettier's article.

The immediate effect of the article was to inspire a search for a special sort of justification that when added to true belief produces knowledge. The justification, it was said, had to be indefeasible or nondefective or in some other way a cut above the ordinary. Others eventually began to search in a different direction, since justification traditionally understood is associated with having reasons that can be used to defend one's beliefs, but in many everyday instances of knowledge, the knower seems not to be in a position to provide such a defense.

Phil knows that the bus is a block away because he sees it, but he would be hard pressed to justify his belief. He knows little about optics or the human visual system. Like other sighted people, he relies upon his eyes for information, but he could not provide a noncircular defense of their overall reliability, and if pressed for such a defense, he would simply become confused. Beth knows that she was at the bank last week because she remembers being there, but she is not able to cite convincing evidence in support of the accuracy of her memory. Margaret knows that the sun is much larger than the earth and that John Wilkes Booth assassinated Lincoln, but she cannot recall the original source of either belief, thus limiting her ability to mount a detailed defense based on the authority of that source. John glimpses a face in a parade and knows it to be that of a childhood friend whom he has not seen for decades, but he has only a vague notion of what visual cues allowed him to recognize his friend.

Examples such as these suggested to many epistemologists that knowledge does not require justification, at least not in a traditional sense, and that to assume otherwise is to overly intellectualize how people acquire much of their everyday knowledge. These epistemologists accordingly shifted their focus away from justification and began to propose accounts, now familiar, in which a true belief, to be knowledge, has to be the product of a highly reliable process, or has to track the truth in close counterfactual situations, or has to be product of cognitive faculties operating in the way that they were designed to function. Because these accounts directed attention away from one's being able to mount "internally" a defense of what one knows and toward causal and causal-like properties, they came to be known as "externalist" accounts of knowledge.

These accounts, in turn, ushered in a new class of externalist accounts of justification. Initially, externalism was part of a reaction against justification-driven theories of knowledge, but an assumption drawn from the old epistemology made it tempting to reconceive justification as well. The assumption is that by definition justification is that which when added to true belief generates a serious candidate for knowledge, with perhaps some fourth condition added to handle Gettier-style counterexamples. If, as many wanted to claim, knowledge is to be understood as something like reliably produced true belief, then relying on the above assumption, it seemed a small step to the conclusion that having justified beliefs at its core must also be a matter of one's beliefs being produced and sustained by reliable cognitive processes.

Such proposals sparked a literature on the relative advantages and disadvantages of externalism and internalism. Much of this literature assumes that externalists and internalists are defending rival theories, but a more charitable reading is that they primarily care about different issues.

Externalists are first and foremost interested in understanding the relationship that has to obtain between one's beliefs and the world in order for the beliefs, when true, to count as knowledge. In carrying out this project, however, they often see themselves as also offering an account of justification, because justification, they presuppose, is that which has to be added to true belief in order to produce a serious candidate for knowledge.

Internalists, on the other hand, are first and foremost interested in understanding what is involved in having beliefs that from one's perspective one is in a position to defend, but they frequently see themselves as also providing the materials for an adequate account of knowledge, because they too presuppose that justification is by definition that which has to be added to true belief to get a serious candidate for knowledge.

This is a presupposition to be resisted, however. As the theories of knowledge and justified belief are independently developed, interesting connections between them may emerge, but the initial and primary focus of the theory of knowledge is different from that of the theory of justified belief. So, it should not be simply assumed from the start that knowledge and justified belief are necessarily linked as opposed to being frequently associated.

Not making this assumption, moreover, is liberating. It frees the theory of knowledge from the uncomfortable choice of either having to embrace an overly intellectual conception of knowledge, which overlooks the fact that people seem not to be in a position to provide adequate intellectual defenses of much of what they know, or having to engage in awkward attempts to force back into the account some nontraditional notion of justified belief, because the definition of knowledge is thought to require it.

Simultaneously, it frees the theory of justified belief from servitude to the theory of knowledge. If it is stipulated that the properties that make a belief justified must be ones that turn a true belief into a good candidate for knowledge, the theory of justified belief is thereby separated from our everyday assessments of each other's opinions, which are more concerned with whether individuals have been appropriately careful and responsible in regulating their opinions than on whether they have satisfied the prerequisites of knowledge.[2]

Once it is no longer assumed that there is a necessary link between justification and knowledge, epistemology is reoriented.

The working strategy that has dominated epistemology since Gettier's article is to employ the assumption that knowledge and justification are conceptually connected to draw strong, and sometimes antecedently implausible, conclusions about knowledge or justification. The strategy can be thought of as an epistemology game. Call it the "Gettier game." It starts with a story in which a subject has a true belief but intuitively seems not to have knowledge, and the play of the game is governed by the rule that justification is one of the conditions that has to be added to true belief in order for it to be a serious candidate for knowledge. The goal is then to identify, within the constraints imposed by this rule, the defect that explains why the subject of the story lacks knowledge.

Solutions to the Gettier game take three forms. First, one can claim that although the subject's belief is true, it is not plausible to regard it as justified. Second, one can claim that although the subject's true belief is justified, it lacks an additional condition (nondefectiveness or indefeasibility or whatever) that has to be present in order for a true justified belief to be an instance of knowledge. Third, one can claim that although at first glance it might seem plausible to regard the subject's belief as justified, the case illustrates why it is necessary to amend the traditional notion of justification; one is then in a position to explain that the subject lacks knowledge because her belief is not justified in the amended sense.

Once the assumption that justification is a necessary condition of knowledge is abandoned, the Gettier game can no longer be played. In its place, however, there is a simpler and more illuminating game to play. The game starts identically, with a story in which a subject has a true belief but intuitively seems not to have knowledge, but it is governed by a different rule: look for some important feature of the situation about which the subject lacks true beliefs.

Except perhaps for a few extreme situations in which knowledge may be blocked, this game always has a solution.[3]

II

Puzzles and Questions

Chapter 10

The Value of True Belief

When knowledge is thought of in terms of adequate information, various puzzles become less problematic, including ones related to the value of true belief and knowledge. In this chapter, I consider issues about the value of true belief, and in the next related issues about the value of knowledge.

Bernard Williams observed that belief is a psychological state that "aims" at truth. John Searle expresses the same point in terms of mind-to-world direction of fit. It is, he says, the "responsibility" of belief to match the world.[1]

Williams and Searle are speaking allegorically—beliefs are not the sort of things that have aims or responsibilities—but the allegories are apt. When we deliberate about what to believe, the value that usually occupies us is truth. We try to determine which beliefs would be true as opposed to which would be useful. We weigh evidence for and against a claim, but we don't very often weigh the practical benefits and costs of believing it as opposed to not believing it.

More precisely, we don't do so explicitly. Self-interest

and other non-truth-related considerations notoriously influence beliefs, but typically not consciously. We rarely make a conscious decision to ignore or discount evidence in favor of a claim because believing it would not be in our self-interest. Deliberations about what to say are of course a very different matter. We often deliberate about whether to say what is polite, useful, or ingratiating as opposed to what is true. Not so with beliefs, however.

Why is this? What a person believes, like what she does, decides, and intends, can have important practical consequences. Yet our practice is by and large not to dwell upon them in deliberations and debates about what to believe. At first glance, this can seem puzzling.

But note, insofar as the context is one in which we are trying to persuade someone (sometimes ourselves) of something, introducing practical considerations is usually beside the point, since ordinarily they are not the kind of consideration that consciously prompts belief.

Suppose one of your goals is to be promoted, but you are skeptical of your chances. Even if I point out to you that believing you will be promoted would make you less nervous which in turn would improve your job performance, thereby making the promotion likely, this ordinarily will not be enough to prompt belief. By contrast, if I cite strong evidence indicating that you will be promoted, belief often does follow.

Deliberating about pragmatic reasons for belief is thus often pointless. It is usually also redundant. Since in general it is in one's interest to have beliefs that are accurate and comprehensive, practical considerations tend to coincide with epistemic ones.

We all are constantly faced with an enormous number of decisions. Some are important while others are less momentous, but even the apparently minor ones, if made badly, can have the potential for disaster, for instance, whether to fasten the seatbelt for a short taxi ride. Moreover, we don't know in advance all the decisions we are going to face and hence don't know what information we will need in order to make them well. This would not matter if we always had ample time to gather information and deliberate, but for the most part we don't. The sheer number of decisions confronting us means that most have to be made on the spot, without the luxury of evidence gathering, consultation, and deliberation. We are forced to draw upon our existing stock of beliefs, and if that stock is either small or inaccurate, we increase the likelihood of poor decisions.

Thus in general, the beliefs most useful to us are those that are accurate and comprehensive. By having such beliefs, we are able to fashion effective strategies for achieving our various ends. Thus, for all practical purposes, taking this phrase literally, we usually can safely restrict our attention to epistemic reasons in our deliberations about what to believe.

To be sure, it is possible to conceive of occasions where epistemic and practical reasons for belief pull in different directions. Pascal famously suggested that belief in God might be such an example, since there is a potentially huge payoff if the belief is true; but it is not difficult to dream up nontheistic examples as well, although the clearest cases again tend to be ones in which the stakes are unusually high. If you are aware that a madman will kill your children unless you come to believe, and not merely act as if you believe, that the earth is flat, you have reasons to find ways of somehow getting yourself to believe this proposition, difficult as this may be. In the vast majority of cases, however, practical considerations push us in the direction of having accurate and comprehensive beliefs. They push us, in other words, in the same direction as our epistemic reasons.

Our normal routine is thus to ignore practical considerations when we are deliberating about what to believe. They do nonetheless extensively influence our opinions. As mentioned above, they do so unconsciously, but more interesting for purposes here is that they also do so in a more calculated and rational way, albeit at one remove. They help determine what issues are worthy of investigation and how much time, energy, and resources it is appropriate to devote to investigating them.

Before starting on a long car trip, I need to decide whether to check the condition of my tires, and if so, how thoroughly to do so. Should I quickly inspect them myself? Should I take the car to a service station and have it put on a lift so that they can be examined systematically? Perhaps I should even take the time to look up the durability record for the make of tires on my car.

Similarly, if I become interested in whether fMRI machines can reliably determine whether a person is lying, I need to decide how much time to devote to looking into this. Should I be content with reading the story published in the science section of the newspaper, or should I also take the time to read the more extensive piece in the recent *New Yorker*, or should I go to the trouble of educating myself about how fMRI machines work?

So it is with countless other issues and questions, from what the balance is in my checking account and what risks are associated with the medication I am taking to which regions of the world have the greatest population growth. I cannot gather evidence and deliberate about every issue that confronts or interests me, much less conduct a thorough inquiry into each. There are too many issues, and my time and capacities are limited. Choices have to be made, and making them well is a matter of gauging how important it is for me to have accurate and comprehensive beliefs about the matter in question. As the stakes go up, so too should my efforts. If it is more important for me to have accurate and comprehensive opinions about P than Q, and if the prospects of successful inquiry are about the same for each, it is reasonable for me to devote more time, energy, and resources to investigating and thinking about P than Q. If I then do so, I am likely to have more extensive and detailed information about P than Q, which in turn shapes what I believe, and what it is rational for me to believe, about each.

Pragmatists in the tradition of James and Dewey sometimes remark that inquiry is or at least ought to be directed at the acquisition of beliefs that are useful. Such remarks underestimate the role of curiosity-driven inquiry, but on the other hand there is often something askance about acquiring truths for their own sake. To return to an example mentioned earlier, if someone spends most of his waking hours going to the houses of friends and counting the number of grains in their saltshakers, he is acquiring truths the rest of us lack, but his project is ill conceived and even disturbing, because it is at odds with a well-ordered life. The value of the information he is acquiring is not commensurate with the time and effort he is expending to obtain it.

So, even if pragmatists sometimes overstate their case, they are on to something. One who counts grains of salt may be acquiring true beliefs, but it is difficult to see how he is acquiring anything of significant value.

This insight can be acknowledged, however, without sliding into the view that the principal goal of deliberation and inquiry is the acquisition of useful as opposed to true beliefs. Practical considerations play a major role in determining what it is reasonable for us to believe, but they do so by helping to determine which issues are worthy of attention and the extent of evidence gathering and deliberation it is appropriate to devote to these issues. They give direction to inquiry and impose constraints on it, but once the direction and constraints are established, usefulness tends to drop out. The aim is then to determine which beliefs would be true, not which would be useful.

Chapter 11

The Value of Knowledge

If the primary aim of inquiry is the acquisition of true beliefs, where does this leave knowledge? Isn't it more valuable than mere true belief? But if so, why? And if knowledge is really more valuable than true belief, does this mean that it rather than true belief should be the primary aim of inquiry? On some accounts of knowledge, it is surprisingly difficult to deal with such questions.

If, for example, justification traditionally understood or some close cousin of it is thought to be the property that turns true belief into knowledge, and if it is assumed, as it often is, that having justified beliefs is valuable because it increases one's chances of having true beliefs, then as a number of philosophers have observed, knowledge would seem to be no more valuable than true belief. If something A is valuable only as a means to B, $A + B$ is not more valuable than B alone.[1]

Suppose, on the other hand, that justification is said to be valuable for its own sake, and it is this that explains why knowledge is more valuable than mere true belief. Problems then arise from a different direction. Having justified beliefs is essentially a matter of putting one's own intellectual house in order. There are different accounts of what this involves, but on any of these views it is problematic to understand why knowledge should be the primary goal of inquiry, since this would seem to make inquiry too self-involved. When one inquires and deliberates about an issue P, the focus shouldn't be on oneself but on acquiring truths about P.[2]

Consider an analogy with ethical motivation. Imagine a philanthropist whose contributions to relief efforts are motivated not by a desire to relieve suffering but rather a desire to be virtuous. This philanthropist is not cynical in the manner of counterfeit do-gooders, that is, those who merely want to be seen as virtuous, but it is still awry, because her focus is on herself as opposed to others. One's intellectual motivations are analogously awry to the degree that one's inquiries and deliberations are aimed at producing beliefs that are justified as opposed to ones that are true.[3]

If the property that turns true belief into knowledge is said not to be justification but the reliability of the faculties or methods that produce the belief, similar problems arise. The most natural construal of why it is valuable to have reliably produced beliefs is that they are likely to be true. But then, a reliably produced true belief P is no more valuable than a true belief P that is not reliably produced. Kobe Bryant on average makes over 80 percent of his free throws, whereas Shaquille O'Neal makes only 50 percent, but a successful free throw by Kobe is not thereby more valuable than a successful one by Shaq.[4]

Each of these accounts is seeking an X distinct from true belief that is capable of turning true belief into knowledge, but in each case the proposed X leads to puzzles or at least awkward questions. Proponents of the accounts try to untangle the puzzles and smooth over the awkwardness,[5] but it is a warning sign that there are problems at all. It ought not to be so difficult to explain both why knowledge is a proper aim of inquiry and why knowing P is usually more valuable than merely having a true belief P.

The view that knowledge is adequate information does better. Much better. There are straightforward ways of explaining both. I say "ways" because the explanation comes in two stages.

To know P, one cannot lack important true beliefs. Thus ordinarily, when one knows P, one has not only a true belief P but also a substantial number of neighboring true beliefs. Why then is knowing P usually more valuable than merely having a true belief P? Because on the assumption that true belief is valuable, one has at least as much and usually more of this valuable commodity when one knows P than when one merely has a true belief P. There is no need to look for something beyond true beliefs to explain why knowledge is usually more valuable than mere true belief. True beliefs themselves provide the explanation.

Similarly, there are no difficulties in explaining why both knowledge and true belief are the aims of inquiry. The two blend into one another. Having true beliefs is the aim of inquiry, and having knowledge is not something distinct from this. It is a matter of having enough true beliefs.[6]

Two additional points, both familiar, need to be folded in to get to the next stage of explanation. The first is that it is more important to have true beliefs about some issues than others, and the second is that the standards of importance are not solely intellectual.

It is, for example, more important to have true beliefs about how cells age than about the number of grains of salt in the saltshakers in the apartments of the Breevoort Building at 11 Fifth Avenue in New York City. As a result, it makes sense to devote more time, energy, and resources to the former than the latter. Yet, the former is neither intrinsically more important than the latter nor more important solely for intellectual reasons. Its greater importance derives rather from its being more closely connected in varied and complex ways with the central values, needs, and purposes of human lives.

In a parallel fashion, the considerations relevant for determining whether S knows P are varied and complex, and include practical as well as intellectual considerations. This can make it difficult to resolve disputes over whether S knows P, but it also points the way to a deeper explanation of the value of knowledge.

If S has a true belief P but does not know, there are important truths she lacks. The kind of importance at issue in assessments of knowledge is importance with respect to having adequate information about the situation in question, where the full range of human concerns and values is potentially relevant in appraising what counts as adequate. In particular, the stakes involved in being right or wrong about P help determine the amount and kind of information S needs in order to have adequate information. There is thus a conceptual link between knowledge and the core concerns of human lives, but no such conceptual link between mere true beliefs and these concerns. It is this difference that most fully explains the differential value of knowledge and true belief.

Consider the point through the lens of the question, why is a set of true beliefs about P that rises to the level of knowledge usually more valuable than an equally large set of true beliefs about P that does not constitute knowledge?[7]

If true beliefs were valuable only by virtue of being either intrinsically valuable or connected with other true beliefs that are intrinsically valuable, there would be no easy answer to this question. If however a set of true beliefs acquires much of whatever value it has through its associations with the various goals, purposes, and needs that make up human lives, and if the concept of knowledge is itself linked to a set of true beliefs having such associations, there is a straightforward answer to this question. If S has a large number of true beliefs about P but they do not constitute knowledge, she lacks truths about P that are important. By contrast, when her beliefs about P rise to the level of knowledge, there are no important gaps in her information about P and hence her beliefs are ordinarily more valuable.[8]

Chapter 12

The Lottery and Preface

Despite surface similarities, lottery and preface cases seem to differ sharply with respect to what is known.

Here is a lottery case. S has bought a ticket in a one-thousand-ticket lottery, and she has compelling evidence that the lottery is fair. The winning ticket, T_{543}, has just been drawn, but no one has yet seen the winning number. S believes that her ticket, T_{345}, is not the winner. Since she is aware there are one thousand tickets and only one winner, she has strong evidence for this belief. Moreover, she is correct. She has not won. Nevertheless, it would seem that she does not know this to be the case.

Here is a comparable preface case. S has written a book on birds in which she makes one thousand independently verified assertions about the size, color, and habits of various species. Although she has meticulously researched each individual assertion, $B_1, B_2 \ldots B_{1000}$, she acknowledges in the preface that she almost certainly has made a mistake or two somewhere. Moreover, she is right; unbeknownst to her, B_{543} is false. Nevertheless, this one mistake would not seem to contaminate her other claims. In particular, it would not seem to preclude her from knowing B_{345}.

The two cases are similar in many ways. S has strong evidence with respect to each ticket in the lottery, including her own, T_{345}, that it is not the winning ticket, and likewise she has strong evidence with respect to each of the claims in her book, including B_{345}, that it is true. She is not aware which of the tickets $T_1, T_2 \ldots T_{1000}$ is the winning ticket and is also not aware which of the claims $B_1, B_2 \ldots B_{1000}$ is false. She believes that T_{345} is not the winning ticket, and it is true that it is not the winning ticket, and similarly she believes that B_{345} is true, and in fact it is. Yet her true belief about T_{345} does not seem to be an instance of knowledge, whereas her true belief about B_{345} does.

Why is this so? Because she seems to lack key information about the former but not the latter. To be sure, there are gaps in her information in both cases. Most notably, in each case she lacks awareness of which proposition in the relevant set is false. In the preface, however, she has extensive documentation of the truth of B_{345} that is distinct from the documentation she has for the other claims in the book, including B_{543}. As a result, her not being aware of the falsity of B_{543} is unlikely to strike us as the kind of gap that prevents her from having adequate information about B_{345}. She can have an adequate grasp of how and why B_{345} is true even though she lacks the information that claims B_{543} is false.

In the lottery, by contrast, she does not have independent evidence that the ticket T_{345} is not the winner. The evidence she has that T_{345} has not won is exactly the same as she has with respect to each of the other tickets that it

has lost, including the winning ticket T_{543}. The propositions of the lottery are in this way more tightly connected
than those of the preface. Correspondingly, not being
aware that T_{543} is the winning ticket is apt to strike us as
an important gap in her information about whether her
ticket T_{345} has or has not won.

The tables are reversed, however, with respect to the
proposition that one of the claims in her book is false and
the corresponding proposition in the lottery that one of
the tickets has won. In the lottery S has strong evidence
that one ticket, she knows not which, is the winning
ticket, and in the preface she has strong evidence that
one of the book's claims, again she knows not which, is
false, but in the lottery she seems to be in a position to
know this proposition, while in the preface she seems not
to be in a position to know the comparable proposition.

The explanation for the difference, once again, is that
the gap in her information tends to strike us as significant in the one case but not the other. In the lottery she
has detailed information about the structure of lotteries
and the fairness of this particular lottery, which in turn
seems to give her adequate information that some ticket
or another has won, even though she isn't aware which
specific ticket is the winner. By contrast, she has no independent and detailed information of how and why it is
that one of the claims in her book is false. She infers that
in all probability that she has made a mistake somewhere,
but she has no details about what kind of mistake it is or
how it was made. It is thus likely to strike us that she
lacks important information about whether she in fact
has somewhere made a mistake.

Chapter 13

Reverse Lottery Stories

Reverse lottery stories, which focus on the fortunate holder of the winning ticket, raise different issues.[1] Here is an example. Imagine again a fair lottery with one thousand tickets. The winning ticket has been selected, but there will be no announcement of the winner until tomorrow. *S* herself did not witness the drawing and has not heard a report from any of those who were present, nor has she seen the script for tomorrow's announcement. She nonetheless believes that she has been lucky and her ticket T_{345} has won. Moreover, she is right. She has in fact won. Despite having a true belief, she does not have knowledge, but what are the important gaps in her information?

There is no shortage of candidates. Had she witnessed the drawing or heard the report of those present or read the script of tomorrow's announcement, she would have been in a position to know, but she hasn't, and hence these gaps are available to explain why she doesn't know.

On the other hand, suppose that no information of this sort is available. No one was allowed to witness the drawing; a secure device was used to select the winning ticket in utter secrecy; and this device was programmed, again with complete security, to generate the announcement tomorrow.

Even so, there are other kinds of information she might have had. If she had somehow been aware of the exact position of her ticket in the drum, the rate of the drum's revolutions, the detailed workings of the device that was used to draw the winning ticket from the drum, and the precise time at which the ticket was drawn, she might have been in a position to know, and not just correctly believe, that her ticket has won. But then, once again, her lacking such information is available to explain why she doesn't know. She lacks knowledge because given the security surrounding the drawing, she has no direct information about which ticket has won, nor does she have detailed enough information about the workings of the drawing to infer that her ticket has won.

Suppose, however, that a random number generator was used to pick the number of the winning ticket. S correctly believes that this is how the winner has been chosen, and she also correctly believes that her ticket has been picked. What then?

If "random" here means what it means in everyday contexts, it does not imply that the outcome could not have been predicted with enough information about initial conditions and the mechanisms used by the number generator but rather that we don't have enough of this information. So, we cannot infer which ticket has been chosen, but in principle someone with sufficiently precise and detailed information could have done so. If the number generator is random in this sense, there again is no shortage of truths S lacks that are available to explain why she doesn't know.

On the other hand, suppose we push the story to its limits by imagining that the processes by which the winning ticket is picked are governed by indeterministic laws, and even relative to full information about these processes and the initial conditions, it is highly improbable that her ticket has won. S correctly believes that the lottery is in this way indeterministic but nonetheless thinks that the improbable has occurred and she has won, and she is right. Even so, she does not have knowledge. Moreover, she would not seem to know regardless how complete a grasp we imagine her having of the initial conditions and relevant mechanisms.

In particular, suppose it is Sally, whose beliefs are maximally accurate and comprehensive, who holds ticket T_{345}. She believes that her ticket has been chosen the winner, and this belief is true. Given the complete security surrounding the drawing, there is no available information about the current situation that would indicate to her that her ticket T_{345} has won. She does have maximally accurate and comprehensive information about prior conditions and the processes used to pick the winning ticket, but this information doesn't put her in a position to infer that she has won. On the contrary, she is aware that relative to this information, it is highly unlikely that she has won. Hence, under these conditions, it would seem that not even Sally knows.

Why is this? Whenever there is a knowledge story far removed from the ordinary, it pays to take a step back in order to assure ourselves, first, that the situation as imagined really is possible and, second, if we judge that it is indeed possible, whether our intuitions about it are the same once we more appreciate in some detail what the situation would look like.

In reexamining the story here, one question that arises is whether its details are inconsistent with the assumption that Sally believes her ticket has won. After all, as the story has been told, she has maximally accurate and complete information about prior conditions and processes, and she correctly believes that relative to this information, it is highly improbable that hers is the winning ticket. But if one believes that a proposition is highly unlikely, it is not obvious that one can simultaneously also be confident enough of its truth to be said to believe it. At the very least, there is enough ambiguity about this to help explain why we are reluctant to grant that Sally has knowledge. It is less than clear that she can know that her ticket has won because it is less than clear that she can even believe this, given that by hypothesis she believes it highly unlikely to be true.

Suppose, however, we were willing to grant for the sake of argument that Sally does in fact believe that her ticket has won. What then? Then there would be another problem, a problem that can make it appropriate to invoke blocking conditions. For under the circumstances now being imagined, Sally's having fully accurate and comprehensive beliefs would involve her having irrational beliefs, since she simultaneously would have to believe both that T_{345} is the winning ticket and also that it is highly improbable that this is so.[2]

Earlier I noted that there may be arguments to the effect that Sally's beliefs couldn't possibly be maximally accurate and comprehensive without also meeting minimum standards of rationality.[3] Here the situation being imagined is reversed; she cannot have maximally accurate and comprehensive beliefs about certain matters without also having highly irrational beliefs about these same matters. But if circumstances are indeed structured in this way, we may want to conclude it is impossible for anyone to know, that knowledge is blocked.

Recall the previous discussion of blocking conditions, which were introduced as a way of dealing with extreme cases. Since intuitions about such cases are apt to be diverse, the suggestion was that blocking conditions be introduced as a way of explaining why a subject might seem to lack knowledge even if she has a true belief and seems not to lack important information. The further suggestion was that blocking conditions be construed in terms of some kind of minimal standard that is not being met. In the beetle in the box story, it was minimal standards of information that were absent. Here in this revised Sally story, it seems to be minimal standards of reasonability.

Chapter 14

Lucky Knowledge

It can be tempting to assume that the explanation for why a subject lacks knowledge in reverse lottery stories must have something to do with its being a matter of luck that she has a true belief about the winning ticket, but this is a temptation to be resisted. What matters is whether her true belief is surrounded by adequate information, not whether she has been lucky.

Here is another lottery-like story to help illustrate this point. Imagine one hundred people in a room, each of whom knows that he or she is about to take part in an experiment. Each will be put into a machine that will make one of the group clairvoyant while providing the other ninety-nine with impressions about the future that are as vivid and convincing as those had by the genuine clairvoyant, only misleading.[1]

After the machine does its work, each subject believes that he or she is the one who has been made clairvoyant, and each also believes that all the other subjects are pseudo-clairvoyant. The lucky subject is S. Like the other ninety-nine, she believes she is clairvoyant, but unlike the others, her belief is true. Still, it might seem that she is not in a position to know she is clairvoyant, but if not, what is the important gap in her information?

Like all stories, this one is selectively incomplete, and there are different ways of filling it in. The story is not explicit, for example, about what information S has about the machine and the experiment. If we fill in the story to make clear that after the machine has turned her into a clairvoyant, she lacks information about how the machine produces clairvoyance in the lucky subject, how it produces pseudo-clairvoyant appearances in the unlucky subjects, and how it is that she became the lucky subject, all these gaps are available to explain why she doesn't have enough information to know she is the clairvoyant one.

On the other hand, suppose we fill in the story so that in the process of becoming clairvoyant, she also acquires detailed and accurate information about all these matters. She has full information about the machine, the experiment, and the conditions that led to her becoming the lucky subject. She thus begins to resemble Sally who has beliefs as comprehensive and accurate as it is possible for a human to have, and it accordingly becomes more plausible to say she knows.

To the degree there is an impression that luck is incompatible with knowledge, it arises because in everyday situations when one luckily acquires a true belief, one commonly does lack knowledge. Recall the original barn case in which George has a true belief that he is looking at a barn, but it is just happenstance that he has stopped his car in front of the few remaining real barns in the region instead of a barn facsimile. As the story has been told, it is a matter of luck that his belief is true, but his being lucky is also correlated with his not being aware that there are nearby barn facades. He is both lucky and ignorant. Blind lucky, as it were.

By contrast, once it is stipulated that S has complete and detailed information about how the clairvoyance machine produces clairvoyance and pseudo-clairvoyance and how it is that she came to be the clairvoyant one, there is still luck involved in her having knowledge, but not blind luck. Like Sally she has all the relevant information.

In a global sense, knowledge always requires good fortune. Brain-in-a-vat stories illustrate that things beyond one's control and awareness can conspire to prevent one from having true beliefs despite one's best efforts. One can be ideally careful and thorough and yet still be deceived. This point is perfectly general. One needs the world to cooperate in order to have knowledge.

The assumption that luck is incompatible with knowledge arises out of the local workings of luck, such as are operative in the barn case. In these cases, however, there is corresponding local ignorance. Remove the ignorance, that is, remove the blindness from the luck, and knowledge becomes possible.[2]

Chapter 15

Closure and Skepticism

Acknowledging that luck is not incompatible with knowledge makes it easier to deal with other puzzles as well.

Consider a variation of the barn story. The story begins like the original: George is touring farm country and is charmed by the old barns he is seeing; he pulls his car over to the side of the road to appreciate the latest he has happened across; and, as he looks out the window, he has a true belief that he is looking at a barn. In this version of the story, however, there are no barn facades in the region. During his tour until now, he has been seeing nothing but real barns. Moreover, he correctly believes that he has normal vision, there is nothing obstructing his view, and the light is good. He thus apparently knows that he is seeing a barn.

Suppose he now recalls the brain-in-a-vat hypothesis, according to which his brain is in a vat in a laboratory where it is being stimulated to produce precisely the sorts of experiences he is now having. He realizes the proposition that he is now looking at a barn entails that he is not a brain-in-a-vat. He accordingly believes this latter proposition, but does he know it?

Well, why not? His belief that he is not a brain-in-a-vat, like his belief that he is looking at a barn, is true, and as the story has been told, there are no obviously important gaps in his information about the situation.

On the other hand, to the degree that one regards it as questionable whether George can know that he is not a brain-in-a-vat, one might be inclined to think that the argument here has to be reversed, with the unwelcome inference being that George cannot even know that he is now seeing a barn.

The basis for such an inference is the principle that knowledge, to use the term of art, is closed under known entailment. According to this principle, if S is aware that A entails B, then S knows A only if she knows B. This is sometimes referred to as "single premise closure," since it applies only to entailments from a single known proposition. A much stronger and correspondingly less plausible principle is that knowledge is closed under multiple premises: if S is aware that (A and B) entails C, then S knows A and knows B only if she knows C. Such a principle, for example, implies that in the preface S cannot know each of individual claims in her book without knowing the conjunction and hence without knowing that she has made no mistakes anywhere in the book. The above argument, however, requires only single premise closure along with the assumption that George does not know that he is not a brain-in-a-vat.[1]

But why make this latter assumption? George's belief that he is not a brain-in-a-vat is true, and as far as we can tell there are no important truths about his circumstances of which he is unaware. So, why isn't his belief an instance of knowledge? One line of argument is that he doesn't have knowledge because knowing something must exclude the possibility of error. Descartes was notoriously attracted to this view, and some notable contemporary philosophers have been drawn to it as well.[2]

This merely pushes the question back a level, however. Why should it be assumed that knowledge has to exclude the possibility of error, especially since most of our everyday attributions of knowledge would seem to suggest the opposite? What is it that is supposed to require such a demanding standard?

The lurking presupposition, once again, would seem to be that knowledge is incompatible with having a true belief by luck. There is nothing from George's perspective that allows him to distinguish a situation in which he is a brain-in-a-vat from one in which he is not. So, even if he correctly believes that he is not a brain-in-a-vat, it is a matter of luck that his belief is true.

But as I have been arguing, not only is knowledge not incompatible with luck, it actually requires it. It requires, in effect, the world to be kind. The inclination to think otherwise derives from a failure to distinguish global from local luck. When one has a true belief as a result of local luck, one usually does lack knowledge, but this is so because the luck is accompanied by local ignorance. In the original barn story, George by happenstance has stopped his car in front of one of the few remaining real barns in the region, and he isn't aware that there are numerous barn facades in the region. His true belief is thus a case of blind luck, but it is his blindness rather than his luckiness that explains his lack of knowledge.

Still, it might be argued that this way of thinking about brain-in-the-vat stories misses their real power, since it approaches the issues from the viewpoint of an audience hearing a story about someone else, in this case George.

To appreciate the force of such stories, one has to entertain them as potentially being about oneself. It has to be treated as a first person problem. What if I, not George, am a brain-in-a-vat? What then?

What then indeed? If contrary to what I believe I am a brain-in-a-vat, then most of my beliefs about my environment are mistaken, and not just in trifling ways but thoroughly and deeply mistaken. I thus know much less than I take myself to know. So much the worse for me, but nothing of great interest follows for the theory of knowledge. To be sure, there are important questions raised by the brain-in-a-vat and other such skeptical hypotheses—in particular, questions about what it is appropriate for me to believe given my perspective—but these are first and foremost questions about justified belief rather than knowledge.

Moreover, among the relevant questions are ones about closure. If I am aware that the proposition that I am now looking at a barn entails that I am not a brain-in-a-vat, am I justified in believing the former only if I am also justified in believing the latter? And if so, can I be justified in believing the latter? Likewise, there are questions about the possibility of error. Can I justifiably believe I am looking at a barn even though I cannot completely exclude the possibility that I am a brain-in-a-vat being stimulated to have experiences of just the sort I would have when looking at a barn?

The answer to each of these questions is yes. Being a brain-in-a-vat would seriously disadvantage me, as would any situation in which I am thoroughly deceived. Allow paranoia free rein in imagining scenarios about hallucinatory drugs, conspiracies, and evil demons. In these scenarios, I am deprived of knowledge, but one of the lessons of such stories is that being thoroughly deceived does not also automatically prevent me from having justified beliefs. Justification is closely associated with what I am entitled to believe, given how things look from my perspective and given that my goal is now to have accurate and comprehensive beliefs. Accuracy is the goal, but not a prerequisite, however. Even in a bubbling vat, it is possible for my beliefs to be justified. I may be a brain-in-a-vat, but I can nonetheless be a brain-in-a-vat with justified beliefs about my environment, including the justified belief that I am not a brain-in-a-vat.[3]

Chapter 16

Disjunctions

Disjunctions create difficulties for many philosophical views. So, it is worth asking whether they create any special problems for the view that knowledge is to be understood in terms of adequate information.[1]

Suppose a fair coin has been flipped and lies covered on the back of S's hand. Let P be that the flipped coin has landed heads and Q that it has landed tails. S does not believe P and does not believe Q, but she does believe (P or Q). Suppose it is P that is true, that is, the coin has landed heads. Although P is a truth that S lacks, we are not likely to regard this as preventing her from knowing the disjunction (P or Q), but why not?

The answer is that even without the information that P is true, S can have adequate information about the truth of the disjunction (P or Q). She is aware that P and Q are only two possibilities here and hence one or the other of them is true. In this respect, the case is analogous to a lottery case, where S knows that the lottery is fair and hence knows that either ticket T_1 or ticket T_2 ... or ticket T_n will be the winning ticket without being aware of which specific ticket will win. Her not being aware which ticket will be the winner need not prevent her from having adequate information about the disjunction's truth, given that she has lots of information about the workings of the lottery and why it is that one of the tickets must be the winner. What would be surprising to her and hence undermining of knowledge is if none of the tickets won, but one of ticket's winning is just what she expects. And so it is with the coin case; S can have enough information to know that either heads has come up or tails has come up without being aware which is true.[2]

Among the lessons here is that it cannot be assumed that if one truth entails another, S's being unaware of the former prevents her from knowing the latter. Conjunctions are the most obvious example. Let A be that Kuala Lumpur is the capital of Malaysia and B that Quito is the capital of Ecuador. The conjunction (A and B) entails A, but if S is aware of the truth of A but not the truth of B, (A and B) is not necessarily the kind of truth we would regard as preventing her from having adequate information about A. We see the connection between the two, of course, but when evaluating whether she knows A, we narrow our focus to it and accept that it is possible for her to know A without believing (A and B).

Disjunctions are merely another instance of this. If P is true and Q is false, then (P or Q) is true, but S's not being aware of P does not necessarily prevent her from having adequate information about the disjunction (P or Q). Once again we see the connection, but we narrow our focus to (P or Q), not the truth P that entails it. Accordingly, as in the coin case, we think that S can have enough information to know (P or Q) even if she is unaware that it is P that is true.

Chapter 17

Fixedness and Knowledge

Suppose *S* believes *P* because of a Ouija board. Even if *P* turns out to be true, she need not know *P*, since there are any number of important truths about *P* and how she came to believe it that she may lack. On the other hand, she may later be in a position to know *P* if she comes to observe its truth firsthand or hears reliable testimony about it or acquires evidence from which she can reasonably infer its truth. A true belief that arrives in the world without the status of knowledge is not fated to be low caste forever.

Imagine, however, that *S* eventually acquires all the relevant, important information about how and why *P* is true, but none of it has any impact on whether or not she believes *P*. The Ouija board has made such an impression on her that her view about *P* is now impervious to change. Had she acquired full information indicating that *P* is false, she would have nonetheless continued to regard it as true. In fact, she acquires full information about its truth, but this information is irrelevant to what she believes about *P*. Moreover, she realizes this. She is aware that her view about *P* has been fixed by the Ouija board and hence has not in any way been influenced by her subsequent evidence.

This is not so easy to conceive. Truths and beliefs about them come in mutually reinforcing clusters. So ordinarily, if one comes to believe all the important neighboring truths indicating P is true, one will also be disposed to believe P. Beliefs are not as isolated from one another as the story would suggest. Indeed, as the story has been told, S's attitude toward P is so fixed and detached from the rest of her belief system that it seems more akin to an obsession or a compulsion than a belief. Her take on P is not subject to the processes of regulation, revision, and influence that govern her other opinions and thus looks more like a rigidified state external to her belief system than something inside it, subject to the give and take of neighboring opinions.

Suppose, however, we set aside these reservations for the moment and postulate that her attitude toward P is one of genuine belief. Does she then know P? By hypothesis she has full information about it and full information as well that her belief is causally sustained by factors unconnected to this information. She is also well aware that in other situations this kind of disconnect from her other opinions would be likely to result in errors, but she has complete information that in her current circumstances there is no such problem. So, why not grant that she has knowledge?

Then again, this is yet another story in which intuitions are not tethered to the familiar and hence are likely to vary. The view that knowledge is adequate information helps explain why.

Insofar as there is felt pull toward knowledge, it is because S has full information about why P is true and how she came to believe it, but insofar we find ourselves reluctant to attribute knowledge to her, it is because strange things are going on with one of the core conditions of knowledge, in this case, the belief condition. Ordinarily, when one has a true belief and also enough information to know, one's belief is neither impervious to change nor isolated from one's other beliefs about the situation. In this story, however, S's mind-set toward P is so fixed and causally detached from what else she believes that it doesn't look like other beliefs, and this helps explains why we may be reluctant to grant she knows. She lacks knowledge because she lacks belief or at least anything resembling ordinary belief.

Chapter 18

Instability and Knowledge

Consider a story that raises issues not of fixedness but instability.

Recall Sally, whose beliefs are as accurate and comprehensive as it is humanly possible for them to be. She has true beliefs about the basic laws of the universe as well as complete as possible information about its history, and using these laws and information, she can explain virtually everything that has happened, is happening, and will happen. Moreover, she has accurate and comprehensive beliefs about how it is that she came to have such accurate and comprehensive beliefs.

Now retell the Sally story so that a demon has instilled these beliefs in her, and every two seconds the demon replaces her true beliefs with massively mistaken beliefs for two seconds. Her belief system is thus the analogue of a blinking light. For two seconds she has maximally accurate and comprehensive beliefs; for the next two seconds she is massively deceived; two seconds later, she once again has accurate and comprehensive beliefs; and so on. During the two-second intervals in which Sally has accurate and comprehensive beliefs, does she have knowledge?[1]

The story is bizarre even by the standards of the evil demon genre. Indeed, so bizarre that it may not be intelligible. Is it really possible for states to blink on and off from moment to moment and still be genuine beliefs? Or is there a degree of volatility that states must not exceed if they are to qualify as beliefs?[2]

Suppose, however, we agree at least for the moment to waive this concern and grant that these are genuine beliefs. During the two-second interval in which her beliefs are completely accurate and comprehensive, does she then have knowledge? To be sure, she will have these true beliefs only for a brief time, but this would not seem to preclude knowledge automatically. It is not impossible to have fleeting moments of insight. I may suddenly understand a logic proof, but I then get interrupted and when I return to the proof, the insight is gone. This does not necessarily mean that I did not have knowledge for a moment.

More exotic examples may be found as well. Think of mystics who claim that some knowledge by its very nature is such that it cannot be sustained. It is too fragile. When every circumstance is right, powerful insight is possible, but when the smallest detail is altered, insight is lost.

If there is mystical knowledge of this sort, it cannot help but be of short duration. The qualification "if" is needed, because the point here is not that the claims of professed mystics are legitimate but rather that their claims to knowledge should not be dismissed as inherently incoherent.

In everyday situations, if one has true but unstable beliefs and is unaware of the source of the instability, this gap in one's information can be used to explain why one lacks knowledge. This is not Sally's situation, however. During the intervals in which the demon is enlightening as opposed to deceiving her, Sally has complete as possible information about the world, including information about how the demon is providing her with all this information and also how this demon will soon be deceiving her. She is fully aware, in other words, of how accurate and comprehensive her beliefs are but also how ephemeral they are.

Demon and brain-in-the-vat hypotheses typically make use of the familiar narrative technique in which the audience is given information that the characters of the story lack. The audience is aware that the characters are being massively deceived, but the characters themselves are not. Sally by contrast does not lack information about her situation that is available to the audience. We the audience thus don't have the standard rationale for denying she has knowledge. On the contrary, we are aware that her information is vastly superior to ours, if only for brief, intermittent periods. Why then shouldn't she be thought of as having knowledge?

On the other hand, intuitions about cases as bizarre as this are apt to vary. It is thus more important to account for the sources of intuitions than insist on any particular one as correct.

Insofar as there is a pull in the direction of knowledge in this kind of case, this is explainable by Sally's having as close to perfect information as it is possible for humans to have, but insofar as there is pull away from knowledge, this too is explainable. Her blinking states are so strange that we may be reluctant to regard them as beliefs, but then, since knowledge requires belief, we also may be reluctant to grant she knows.

It is possible, of course, to retell the story so that the alternating moments of enlightenment and ignorance are extended from two seconds to, say, two weeks or two months or even two years. If so, we are likely to be more comfortable in regarding them as genuine beliefs, but correspondingly it will then also seem less problematical to grant that she has knowledge during the periods of enlightenment.

Chapter 19

Misleading Defeaters

Once the assumption that justification is a necessary component of knowledge is discarded, the Gettier game can no longer be played. In its place, I have recommended a different game: when a subject has a true belief but seems not to have knowledge, look for some key aspect of the situation about which the subject lacks true beliefs.

Defeasibility theorists make a strikingly similar recommendation. When confronted with cases in which a subject intuitively lacks knowledge despite having a justified true belief, they too recommend looking for a truth about the situation that the subject lacks, but because they are committed to the Gettier game, they link the subject's ignorance of this truth with the justification requirement. The subject lacks knowledge, they say, because the missing truth, if believed, would defeat the subject's justification for the target belief. But once the link between justification and knowledge is severed, as it should be in any event,[1] a simpler explanation is possible. The subject lacks knowledge because she isn't aware of an important truth.

Consider a story discussed by Peter Klein, a leading proponent of the defeasibility theory.[2] Loretta has been working on her federal taxes. She has followed the procedures on the forms carefully, done the calculations meticulously, and as a result correctly believes she owes $500. She is nonetheless worried that she may have made an error. So, she has asked her accountant to verify her return. The accountant has done so and has found no errors, but in writing to Loretta he inadvertently leaves out the word "no," so that his letter reads, "Your return contains errors." Loretta has received the letter but not yet opened it. It lies unread on Loretta's desk.

Loretta has a justified true belief that she owes $500, and despite the fact that there is a truth that would defeat the justification for her belief (the truth that the letter from her accountant contains the sentence "Your return contains errors"), we are inclined, says Klein, to grant she has knowledge. But if so, defeasibility theorists have a problem, as Klein himself recognizes. The problem can be solved, he argues, by introducing a distinction between genuine and misleading defeaters. Although reading the letter from her accountant would defeat the justification for her belief, Loretta nonetheless knows that she owes $500, because the defeating truth here is misleading.

Of course, this merely pushes the problem back a level, the question now being, what distinguishes misleading from genuine defeaters? Klein's answer, some details aside, is that a defeater is misleading if it justifies a falsehood in the process of defeating the justification for the target belief. In the case here, the falsehood is that the accountant had in fact discovered an error in going over Loretta's return.

By contrast, if knowledge is viewed as adequate information, the critical question to ask about this story is, how important is the gap in Loretta's information? As with other stories in the post-Gettier literature, we the audience are given information that the subject Loretta lacks, in this case that the unopened accountant's letter states that there are errors in her return. Is this gap significant? Well, if she had read the letter, she would not have been as convinced as she is now that she owes $500. So, the letter is not beside the point, but had she read the letter, what would have happened next? One likely scenario is that she would have called her accountant and asked what the errors were, at which point she would have discovered that his letter contains a typo. In other words, on one natural expansion of the story, indeed, the very expansion that lies behind the intuition that Loretta knows, had she read the letter, this would have prompted her to acquire additional information that would have quickly countered the misleading sentence in the letter.

On the other hand, there are alternative ways of expanding any story, and with the story here, some of the expansions would raise the significance of the gap in Loretta's information. Suppose her accountant is now on vacation and thus, had she opened the letter and called her accountant's office, she would have spoken to the office administrator, who, let us further stipulate, would have told her that the accountant is always extremely careful in writing such letters. If pressed by Loretta for details, the administrator would have called the accountant on vacation, who having just finished working on scores of returns would not have remembered the details of Loretta's, but he would have instructed his administrator to reassure Loretta that he is always extremely fastidious in preparing his responses and thus whatever he wrote in his note is almost certainly accurate.

As the story is expanded in this direction, some listeners may be pulled away from the intuition that Loretta knows she owes $500. But if so, defeasibility theorists will need to explain why. What is the genuine defeater? Is there some additional factor in the revised story that turns the relevant truth here (the truth that the letter from the accountant contains the sentence "Your return contains errors") from a misleading defeater into a genuine defeater, or is there perhaps another, more complicated truth that defeats her justification without justifying a falsehood?

Defeasibility theorists may be able to patch together answers to such questions,[3] or they may choose simply to dig in their heels and insist that in both expansions of the story, it is clear that Loretta has knowledge. Be this as it may, there is a simpler and more direct way to treat these cases. Namely, the first expansion of the story makes Loretta's missing information seem relatively trivial, whereas the second makes it appear more serious. In particular, the first expansion is such that the misleading sentence in the unopened letter, had Loretta read it, would have been easily and quickly corrected, whereas in the second expansion this is pointedly not the case. On the contrary, reading the letter would have resulted in her obtaining additional confirmation that the letter as written is correct. The gap in her information thus begins to look more significant, and as a result there may be a corresponding pull away from knowledge.

Chapter 20

Believing That I Don't Know

When *S* knows *P*, there are no important truths about the situation she lacks, but is the truth that she knows *P* itself an important truth about the situation? If it were, then in order to know *P*, she would have to believe that she knows it.

This is not a requirement, however. The kind of importance relevant to assessments of knowledge is importance with respect to the subject's having adequate information, where both intellectual and practical considerations can play a role in determining what counts as adequate. The truth that *S* knows *P*, however, need not strike us as being important for either her role as an inquirer about *P* or her role as an agent who might rely on *P*. There may be some special situations in which we expect her to have this meta-belief, but not in general. She can have adequate information about *P* and hence know *P* without necessarily being aware that she knows it.

More intriguing for the theory of knowledge are cases in which we believe something to be true but readily admit we don't know it. Beliefs outside our areas of expertise are commonly like this. I believe that a sidereal day is shorter than a solar day, but my expertise in astronomy is shallow enough that I wouldn't be comfortable representing myself as knowing this. And even within one's area of expertise, beliefs about complex issues are frequently of this sort. If I am a meteorologist with a specialty in hurricanes, I may believe that the hurricane now forming in the Atlantic will pass north of the Leeward Islands, because I have studied the predictive models and they all agree on this, but given the complexity of factors affecting the paths of hurricanes, I may be reluctant to claim knowledge.

The knowledge stories of contemporary epistemology are typically third-person stories in which the storyteller has information that the subject of the story lacks. By contrast, when I report that I believe but don't know P, I am gesturing at an autobiographical story, one in which I am simultaneously storyteller and subject of the story. There is thus no possibility of the storyteller being aware of information that the subject lacks.

Even so, there is nothing puzzling about such reports. When I acknowledge that I believe but don't know P, I am commenting on my lack of surrounding information. My focus is not so much directly on P—I think I have that right—as on neighboring truths. I realize that my grasp of the overall situation in which P is true is sketchy enough that there are many gaps in my information, some of which may well be important. I am thus reluctant to claim knowledge.[1]

It is not as simple, however, for other accounts of knowledge to explain why such reports are so common. Consider reliability theories. To believe P is to believe that P is true, and thus insofar as I am aware that I believe P, I tend to think that reliable processes have produced my belief. But then, if knowledge is basically a matter of having reliably produced true beliefs, when I believe P and am aware of my belief, my default assumption should be that I know P. This isn't my default assumption, however.

There is an analogous issue for justification theorists. When I believe P and am aware that I believe it, I ordinarily think that I have better reasons to believe it than either to disbelieve it or to withhold judgment on it. But insofar as justification is thought to be the key ingredient that lifts true belief into the category of knowledge, it again seems as if my default assumption should be that I also know P, but it isn't.

Reliability and justification theorists may be able to come up with ways of explaining why reports of the form "I believe but don't know P" are common,[2] but there is no need even to search if knowledge is understood in terms of true belief plus adequate information. There is an immediately obvious explanation. When I believe P and am aware that I believe it, I am pressured, given the nature of belief, to think there is nothing amiss with my belief —it is true, reliably produced, justified, etc.—but I am in no way pressured to think that there are not other important truths about the situation of which I am unaware.

Chapter 21

Introspective Knowledge

In everyday contexts it sounds odd to say of someone that she believes she has a headache, and equally odd to say she knows. This has encouraged some philosophers to conclude that it is inappropriate to talk of either belief or knowledge in such cases.[1]

An alternative diagnosis, however, is that the "owner" of a headache is in such a superior position compared with others with respect to determining whether she herself has a headache that it is usually enough to say of her that she has a headache and unnecessary, and hence odd sounding, to add that she believes or knows this.

What exactly is this superior position? Some philosophers maintain that first-person beliefs about headaches are infallible; S cannot believe that she has a headache without understanding what a headache is, but insofar as she understands what a headache is, she cannot be mistaken about whether she has one.[2] Others disagree, arguing that belief acquisition always involves background assumptions and hence it is always possible for things to go wrong, but S's beliefs about her own headaches do at least have a positive presumptiveness about them.[3] Still others make the point that headaches are among the psychological states that automatically reveal themselves to their owners. Timothy Williamson's term for such states is "luminous," while Roderick Chisholm's is "self-presenting."[4]

Whatever their other differences, however, virtually everyone concedes that S has an awareness of her own headaches that others lack, an awareness that involves a special access to the headache's defining characteristic, namely, its unpleasant quality. Her beliefs about her own headaches are thus different in kind from the beliefs that others can have about her having a headache. It is this that accounts for the much tighter than usual link between belief and knowledge.

Recall the beetle in the box story, in which S has a true belief that there is a beetle inside the box but lacks knowledge, but not because she is unaware of available information. It is the world, not S, that has the defect. The world is so informationally impoverished with respect to the box that it is not possible for anyone to know that there is a beetle inside.

The beetle story is the reverse of cases involving awareness of one's own headaches. There are no important truths about the box that others have and S lacks, and yet she seems not to know that there is a beetle inside the box. By contrast, if S has a true belief that she has a headache, there can be any number of truths about the headache that others have and she lacks, for example, ones about its etiology. These truths are nonetheless unlikely to be grounds for denying that she knows, given that she has a special access, an access that others of necessity lack, to its characteristic unpleasantness.

In all but a few unusual situations in which knowledge is blocked, when S has a true belief P but we are nonetheless inclined to say she does not know P, we are aware of something important about the situation that she doesn't "get," but with respect to her own headaches, we realize that the key feature of the headache is precisely the feature she gets all too well. First-person beliefs about headaches thus tend to be instances of narrow knowledge. Little information beyond awareness of the headache itself is relevant to whether she has adequate information, not even information that is noteworthy with respect to other purposes. Suppose the headache is being caused by a tumor that if left untreated would cause her serious health problems. We the audience are aware of this, but S is not. This is clearly a consequential truth, but we are nonetheless not likely to regard it as precluding her from having adequate information about the fact that she has a headache. Like other cases of narrow knowledge, little matters beyond the truth of her belief.

More precisely, this is so with respect to first-person, present tense beliefs about headaches. Beliefs about one's own past and future headaches, even if true, do not so readily qualify as knowledge, because these beliefs, being about the past and future, do not involve a special access to the defining unpleasant quality of the headache. So, additional information can be relevant, just as it is in assessing whether one knows that someone else has a headache.[5]

Nor need first-person, present tense beliefs about other kinds of psychological states be cases of narrow knowledge. Think of states less closely connected with a distinctive sensation and more closely associated with telltale patterns of behavior, for example, jealousy, envy, and fear, and states involving propositional attitudes (what one believes, hopes, intends, wants, and so on).

There is more room for observers to think that the owner lacks key information about these kinds of states, and hence more room to deny that she has knowledge.

A simple way to illustrate this is to consider the role that others can play in getting the owner to be aware that she is in such a state. Consider envy. Others can observe envious patterns in S's behavior and point them out to her. If S herself has been unobservant of these patterns, she can be genuinely surprised to discover that she is envious. Correspondingly, when she is not envious, she can have a true belief to this effect and yet not know it, because once again she may not have been sufficiently attentive to her own behavior.

Chapter 22

Perceptual Knowledge

In the 1988 film *Rain Man*, inspired by the autistic savant Kim Peek, Dustin Hoffman plays a character, Ray, who has unusual talents as well as unusual defects. One of his talents is that without counting he can visually ascertain the number of objects in large sets. In a memorable scene, a box of toothpicks spills on the floor of a restaurant. He looks at the spill for an instant and declares "82, 82, 82." His brother Charlie, played by Tom Cruise, dismisses Ray, saying that there are far more than 82 toothpicks on the floor. Ray immediately responds, "A total of 246." A waitress looks into the overturned toothpick box and observes that there are 4 toothpicks left in the box that held 250. Without counting the individual toothpicks, Ray has visually divided the spill into three groups of 82 and determined that the total is 246.

The film is constructed to suggest to viewers that Ray knows that there are three groups of 82 toothpicks on the floor. Previous scenes have drawn attention to the fact that although he has emotional problems and lacks common sense, he also has rare intellectual abilities. The cumulative effect of these scenes is to raise the salience of his unusual talents and the curious ways he deploys them. For example, early in the restaurant scene, when the waitress who later spills the toothpicks arrives at Ray and Charlie's table, she is wearing a nametag with the name "Sally Diggs" and no other information. Ray glances at the nametag and says, "Diggs, Sally. 4610192." The waitress is taken aback and warily asks, "How do you know my phone number?" Ray responds nonchalantly that the previous night he had memorized the local phone book through to the letter *D*.

This scene and others like it alert the audience that Ray has remarkable intellectual abilities, is aware of these abilities, and makes his own idiosyncratic uses of them. So, when he observes without counting that there are three sets of 82 toothpicks on the floor, it is natural for the audience to assume he has reliably made such determinations in the past and he realizes he has this ability. This assumption is corroborated when the audience sees Ray register no surprise when Sally confirms that there are in fact 246 toothpicks on the floor. He takes it for granted that he was correct.

We are sometimes reluctant to concede that someone knows *P* if he is unaware of how he gets information about matters such as *P* or lacks information about whether he has been reliable about such matters in the past.[1] The scenes in *Rain Man*, however, are arranged to suggest that there are no gaps of this sort in Ray's information. On the contrary, he seems as aware of and as comfortable with his ability to determine by quick visual inspection the number of objects in large sets as the rest of us are with respect to small sets (four books on the table, three people in line, two chairs in the corner).

A lack of awareness about how one acquires information or one's track record of reliability is sometimes the kind of gap that can preclude one from knowing even if one has relatively complete information, but the reverse is also true. A working familiarity with the source of one's belief P coupled with an awareness of the source's reliability can sometimes help make up for a relative lack of information about P itself.

Beliefs based on testimony often display this compensatory quality. If S believes that the Yankees won last night's game because a trusted friend who is close follower of baseball has told her so, her belief may well be an instance of knowledge even if she has relatively few details about the game. Familiarity with the reliability of a source of information about P can relax the demands for additional information about P itself.

The same dynamic is commonly at play with perceptual beliefs. The waitress comes to know by quick visual inspection that there are four toothpicks left in the box, and Ray comes to know by quick visual inspection that there are three groupings of eighty-two toothpicks on the floor. Neither Ray nor the waitress need be aware of much additional information about the toothpicks—for example, whether they are made of plastic or wood or whether they belong to the restaurant or an employee or whether they have been on the shelf for only several hours or several weeks. Additional information is especially not needed if we assume that they have a working familiarity with their histories of reliability, in the waitress's case her history of reliability in perceptually determining the number of objects in small sets and in Ray's case his history of reliability in perceptually determining the number of objects even in large sets.

Perceptual beliefs that are the products of cursory visual inspection are in this respect similar to memory beliefs that are the products of immediate recall. When asked the date of the Battle of Marathon, a contestant on a quiz show confidently and immediately remembers from her high school history course that the date is 490 BCE, but she cannot recall that the Greeks won the battle or even that the adversaries were the Greeks and Persians. Still, it may strike us that whatever else she does or does not know about the battle, she at least knows its date, since the story been told to focus attention on the importance of her being able to answer a specific question, what is the date of the Battle of Marathon?[2] If in addition the story is constructed to suggest she has a history of reliability with respect to remembering dates and she is aware of this history, we will be all the more inclined to relax expectations about how much additional information she needs in order to know.

In a similar way, the scene of Ray in the restaurant is constructed to focus attention on a narrow question (how many toothpicks are on the floor?), and we are led to believe Ray has a working familiarity with the unusual ability that allows him to answer this question. So, as in the case of *S*'s remembering the date of the battle, it strikes us that whatever else he may or may not know about the toothpicks, he at least knows that there are three groups of eighty-two of them on the floor.

Chapter 23

A Priori Knowledge

Some kinds of knowledge are not readily understandable in terms of adequate information if for no other reason than they seem not to be linked with specific truths. Knowledge of people, places, and things and knowledge how are examples.

S knows Jimmy Carter from the time she spent working in the White House. She lived for a year in an apartment near the Eiffel Tower and in that year came to know the seventh arrondissement of Paris. She regularly sees her boss in the firm's parking lot and hence knows his car. In addition, she knows how to ski, how to use the London underground, and how to rewire an electrical socket.

For *S* to have such knowledge, she no doubt needs to believe various truths, but there is no single, particular truth she has to believe. By contrast, for *S* to know that Jimmy Carter was the thirty-ninth president of the United States or that Paris is the capital of France, the truth that has to be believed is straightaway evident.

There may be ways of arguing that despite initial appearances, knowledge how and knowledge of people, places, and things are always identified with specific true beliefs, and at bottom are even species of knowledge that.

It requires ingenious arguments to defend such views, however,[1] whereas with factual knowledge, the connection with at least one believed truth is immediate and obvious. S knows that P only if she believes P and P is true.

A priori knowledge is sometimes thought to be a species of knowledge requiring separate treatment, but unlike knowledge how and knowledge of people, places, and things, when S knows something a priori, there is a readily identifiable truth she believes. She knows a priori that $2 + 3 = 5$ only if she has a true belief that $2 + 3 = 5$; she knows a priori that every square is a rectangle only if she has a true belief that every square is a rectangle; and so on. There is thus a foothold for understanding a priori knowledge in terms of adequate information.

The a priori is to be distinguished from the necessary. A proposition's being known a priori does not ensure that it is necessary, nor does a proposition's being necessary ensure that it can be known a priori. Nevertheless, the paradigmatic examples of a priori knowledge are of necessary truths, for example, truths of arithmetic, truths of logic, and conceptual truths.

As with contingent truths, it is possible for S to believe a necessary truth but not know it, and the explanation is also the same, namely, there are important truths of which she is unaware. With necessary truths as with contingent ones, there are inevitably gaps in S's understanding. The relevant question is whether the gaps are important enough to keep her from knowing.

Consider the theorem that the area inside a circle is equal to that of a right triangle whose base is equal to the circumference of the circle and whose height is equal to its radius. Suppose S believes this theorem. Although her belief is true, we may be reluctant to grant that she knows the theorem if she is not aware that the circumference of a circle is $2\pi r$, or that the formula for calculating the enclosed area of a circle is $\pi r 2$. There is too much important neighboring information she lacks.

By contrast, with the simplest of necessary truths, such as $2 + 3 = 5$, little may be required for knowledge beyond belief. Insofar as S doesn't believe the truths most immediately in the neighborhood, for example, the truth that $5 - 3 = 2$, it becomes doubtful whether she really understands and hence really believes the proposition that $2 + 3 = 5$.[2] On the other hand, related but more distant truths—for example, many of the theorems of number theory—don't seem critical. S can be unaware of them and yet still seem to have enough information to know that $2 + 3 = 5$. Stories involving beliefs about very simple necessary truths thus tend to be stories of narrow knowledge, with the truth that is the center of attention overshadowing associated truths.

Chapter 24

Collective Knowledge

The difference between individual and collective knowledge is the difference between individual belief and collective acceptance. Just as an individual knows *P* if she believes *P*, *P* is true, and there is no important gap in her information about *P*, so too *P* belongs to the collective stock of knowledge of a group of individuals if *P* is collectively accepted by the group, *P* is true, and there is no important gap in the group's collective information about *P*.

Although two kinds of knowledge have the same structure, there are complex questions about their relationship. Some of these questions revolve around the constitution of the groups that can collectively accept and, if all goes well, collectively know something. How narrow or broad can these groups be? Can a group as large as all the people currently alive be said to have collective knowledge of something? What about a group as narrow as the members of a single household? And, how loosely organized can a group be and yet still collectively accept and know something? Is it possible for all individuals with green eyes to have collective knowledge? Or do the individuals have to be spatially, temporally, or culturally linked in characteristic ways? If so, what are these ways?

Intriguing as such questions are, for purposes here the most pressing questions are ones about the relationship between collective acceptance by a group and the beliefs of the individuals making up the group, however that group is defined. Collective acceptance and individual beliefs, and hence collective knowledge and individual knowledge, are linked but not as straightforwardly as one might initially suppose.

The simplest way for a claim to be collectively accepted by a group (community, society, etc.) is for enough individuals within the group to believe the claim, but collective acceptance is not always a matter of sheer numbers. Even when only a few individuals believe a claim, it can nonetheless become collectively accepted and known, provided these individuals have the requisite intellectual standing within the group.

This is a particularly important point in our era of intellectual specialization, where experts have rapidly expanded the collective stock of knowledge and have done so in fields so specialized that only a very few highly trained individuals are in a position to understand, much less evaluate, the propositions in question. Public assertions of a proposition P by highly trained experts can nonetheless lead to collective acceptance and knowledge if others are prepared to defer to them. The "others" here include not only nonexperts but also other experts who begin to rely on P in their own investigations.[1]

The phenomenon of experts relying on the work of other experts is an important aspect of the symbiotic relationship that exists between individual and collective knowledge. Intellectual breakthroughs in a specialized field by a few individuals can add to the collective stock of knowledge, which lays the groundwork for further advances by other individuals in the field itself but also in related fields, which in turn can lead to yet additional growth in collective knowledge, and so on.

The discoveries of Copernicus in the sixteenth century, Kepler in the seventeenth, Lavoisier in the eighteenth, Maxwell in the nineteenth, and Einstein in the twentieth were possible only because previous investigators had built up collective stocks of knowledge that these investigators made ingenious uses of. Their discoveries then added to the collective store of knowledge, thus putting future investigators in an improved position to make yet further discoveries.

As these examples suggest, collective knowledge is especially important in science. C. S. Peirce famously argued that the collective nature of scientific inquiry is an essential component of scientific rationality. His argument, briefly stated, was that unless individual scientists had trust in the community of future inquirers and saw themselves as a part of this community, there would be little point to their work. There would be little point, he thought, because the goal of scientific inquiry is nothing less than a complete and final account of whatever is being investigated, but given the relatively early stage of human intellectual history and the relative shortness of human lives, it is not realistic for individuals on their own to achieve this goal, at least not for topics of significance. Peirce thus concluded that individual scientists must, as a condition of rationality, view themselves as part of a temporally extended community of inquirers, a community that will continue its work well into the future. For it is only by identifying oneself with such a community and by focusing on one's role in increasing collective knowledge that one has a realistic chance of achieving the principal intellectual goal in doing science, namely, a final, fixed treatment of the topic one is investigating.[2]

It is questionable whether the aim of scientific inquiry cannot be anything less than a complete and fixed account of what is being investigated, as Peirce presupposes, but this presupposition aside, he is on to an important point. Despite the remarkable achievements of individual scientists, science is at its heart a collective enterprise, albeit a collective enterprise driven forward by individual effort and achievement.

The key mechanism for incorporating individual achievement into the collective enterprise is the division of intellectual labor. Reduced to its bare bones, the system works by breaking problems into components, providing incentives for investigators to develop highly refined expertise in these narrowly defined components, and requiring them to make available to other investigators the specialized information they acquire.

The signs of ever-increasing specialization in the sciences are everywhere. One is no longer a specialist in physics but rather a specialist in theoretical high-energy physics, or even more specifically in string theory. Similarly, one is not so much a life scientist as a molecular biologist and not so much a molecular biologist as a molecular geneticist.

A widely noted consequence of this ever more fine specialization is that nonspecialists, even highly educated ones, lack the background needed to assess work being done in specialized fields. An authority on Renaissance literature is not in a position to evaluate the latest developments in string theory.

This is the point that so worried C. P. Snow with his reference to "the two cultures" of the sciences and the humanities.[3] What is less widely noted is that fellow scientists are not in a much better position. Biologists lack the training and background required to evaluate developments in string theory, and for that matter so do most other physicists. Similarly, string theorists are not especially well positioned to assess recent developments in molecular genetics, and neither are geologists or condensed matter theorists.

There is a reinforcing dynamic at work here. The division of intellectual labor and the accompanying increased specialization of knowledge produce a vastly expanded stock of collective knowledge, but this vastly expanded stock in turn makes further specialization increasingly inevitable because it is no longer feasible for even the brightest, most encyclopedic individual to master even a small fraction of that which is collectively known.

There is no point bemoaning this trend. It is the to-be-expected consequence of the above dynamic with its emphasis on collective knowledge. One of the most important changes in intellectual life over the past several hundred years is the increasingly large gap between individual knowledge and the collective stock of knowledge. Moreover, the gap is widening even for the most highly educated.

Consider a leading contemporary scientist, the physicist Steven Hawking, for example. Drawing upon work of multiple generations of previous physicists, Hawking has a far more accurate and comprehensive understanding of the physical world than did Archimedes, DaVinci, Galileo, or Newton. On the other hand, Archimedes, DaVinci, Galileo, and Newton had knowledge of a greater percentage of the collective knowledge of their eras than Hawking has of the collective knowledge of our time. Not because Hawking is any less bright, energetic, or curious. The explanation, rather, is that individual scientific knowledge cannot keep pace with increases in collective scientific knowledge.

The widening gap between individual and collective knowledge has major social, political, and educational implications, and given its centrality, it is still underappreciated. I too, however, will be sidestepping the issue, since the key issue for purposes here is that science at its heart is a collective enterprise. In recent years, observations about the social dimensions of science have tended to be prefatory to raising doubts about its claims to objectivity, but this is not my point. Mine is the claim that science is a social enterprise in the sense that its central aim is the expansion of collective knowledge.

On the other hand, the principal tool for accomplishing this aim is the division of intellectual labor, which encourages individual scientists to acquire extraordinarily detailed information about the components of larger scientific problems so as to minimize the likelihood of there being important gaps in their understanding of these component issues. This is just to say that it encourages the acquisition of individual knowledge in the service of collective knowledge.

III

The Structure of Epistemology

Chapter 25

A Look Back

I have repeatedly urged caution about the practice, common in contemporary epistemology, of using tiny stories to elicit intuitions about knowledge, but I have resisted taking the next step and declaring a "pox" on the entire practice. Perhaps in part out of conservatism or even sentimentality—I too was trained in the practice—but also, I trust, for less complacent reasons. I have been trying to illustrate that there is a project worth doing that makes use of stories and the intuitions they produce, but it is a project in which the constant refrains are "not so fast" and "not so sure."

Not so fast and not so sure because it is not enough to spin out little stories and then ask what the intuitions about them are. The stories have too few details; there are too many ways to expand them; they not infrequently describe circumstances far removed from the ordinary; and storytellers can shape them to encourage the reactions they seek. Intuitions about the stories are not clean data. Nor are they even uniform. They vary from person to person and occasion to occasion. Moreover, when they conflict, the complexity of factors affecting them can make it difficult to resolve the dispute.

My strategy, therefore, has been to go up a level where the aim is to explain knowledge intuitions as opposed to relying on them as data. Rather than huffing and puffing about which intuitions are correct, the spirit is ecumenical. The task is more about shedding light on what is causing the conflicting intuitions than choosing among them.

I have also been guided by a yearning to keep things simple when it comes to theorizing about knowledge, and in particular to keep in mind that the primary aim of inquiry is to acquire truths, especially ones that matter. It would be convenient if there were a mark that announced to us when we have succeeded in uncovering truths. We could then declare beliefs with this mark as the winners, the ones worthy of the accolade "knowledge." It is such a mark that Descartes and other prominent figures in the history of epistemology sought, but that history teaches us that there are no such marks. Beliefs do not wear truth on their sleeves. The lesson of the brain-in-a-vat is that no matter how carefully and thoroughly we deploy our capacities, there can be no assurances that the resulting beliefs are true, nor even assurances that they are mostly true. We thus have no choice but to live with intellectual uncertainty, to live without guarantees that our opinions have the property we most seek. We are working without a net.[1]

But if there can be no question of equating knowledge with beliefs that are branded with a mark of their own truth, let's make things simpler. Let's not insist that knowledge be a vessel that contains a desideratum related to true belief but distinct from it—something to do with its justification or pedigree, for example. Let's instead say that knowledge is a matter of having enough true beliefs and then get on with the enterprise of attempting in our fallibilistic ways to determine what is true and what is not.

I'm aware of how provocative this view is. It stands in opposition to a long venerable tradition in epistemology. Although I have acknowledged that when true beliefs rise to the level of knowledge, they usually have many of the merits that the tradition holds most dear, I have insisted that these merits are frequent accompaniments of knowledge, not prerequisites. If S has a true belief P and there is no important gap in her information, then except in a few unusual situations in which knowledge may be blocked, she knows P. Nothing more is required.

In the final two chapters, I sketch some of the ways in which this approach to knowledge fits within a complete epistemology.

Chapter 26

Epistemology within a General Theory of Rationality

The history of epistemology in large part can be read as an attempt to come to grips with two questions, what is it to have justified beliefs, and what is it to have knowledge? Parts 1 and 2 have been concerned with the latter question, but a complete epistemology needs also to address the former as well as the relationship between the two.

Chapter 9 provides some of the groundwork. Once the assumption that justified belief is a necessary condition of knowledge is abandoned, the Gettier game can no longer be played, and the way is cleared for a reorientation of epistemology. This chapter and the following one sketch this reorientation.

But first, a brief review of some relevant history. Throughout much of modern epistemology, the working assumption has been that there is a necessary connection between justified belief on the one hand and true belief and knowledge on the other. A traditional view is that justified beliefs are ones arrived at using an appropriate methodology, where an appropriate methodology guarantees truth.

Descartes, for example, argued that if one restricted oneself to believing only that which is impossible to doubt, one would be assured of not falling into error. Locke's position was only slightly less optimistic. He maintained that one's degree of confidence in a proposition ought be proportionate to the strength of one's evidence, in which case the propositions in which one had a high degree of confidence would be mostly true.

Neither Descartes nor Locke, however, could keep justified belief securely linked with true belief and knowledge without invoking God as the guarantor. Descartes insisted that God would not permit us to be deceived about that which we cannot doubt, while Locke claimed that if we use our perceptual faculties and faculty of reason properly, our general reliability is assured, since God created these faculties.

Contemporary epistemologists are not as inclined to deploy theological assumptions to solve epistemological problems, but they too have been reluctant to abandon the assumption that justification and knowledge are necessarily connected. So, semantic stipulation has replaced theology as a way of ensuring the link. Knowledge is said by definition to involve justified belief.

On this view, the direction of the link is reversed from that sought by Descartes and Locke. Having justified beliefs does not guarantee true belief or knowledge. The idea, rather, is that because knowledge is to be defined as justified true belief, knowing P entails that the belief P is justified.

I have been arguing, however, that it is a mistake to stipulate in advance that there has to be a necessary tie between justified belief and knowledge. The theories of justified belief and knowledge have very different initial foci, and as such the working presupposition should be that the theories are distinct. Separate and equal, as it were. Moreover, as discussed in chapter 9, the separation brings benefits to both parties.

It frees the theory of knowledge from the dilemma of either having to insist on an overly intellectual conception of knowledge, according to which one is able to provide an intellectual defense of whatever one knows, or straining to introduce a nontraditional notion of justified belief because the definition of knowledge is thought to require this.

It simultaneously frees the theory of justified belief from servitude to the theory of knowledge, a servitude that makes it difficult for the theory of justified belief to be relevant to our everyday assessments of each other's opinions, which tend to focus on whether one has been appropriately thorough and careful in formulating one's one opinions as opposed to whether one has satisfied the prerequisites of knowledge. If the properties that make a belief justified are stipulated to be ones that turn a true belief into a good candidate for knowledge, the theory of justified belief has no choice but to be concerned with the latter.

There are other benefits. The concept of justified belief ought to be closely linked with that of rational belief, which in turn ought to be strongly tied to our ways of understanding the rationality of actions, decisions, strategies, plans, etc. But if justified belief is joined to knowledge, then so too will rational belief, and the more closely rational belief is coupled with the prerequisites of knowledge, the more estranged it becomes from our ways of understanding the rationality of other phenomena. The result is that questions about the rationality of beliefs get treated as if they were somehow fundamentally different from questions about the rationality of actions, decisions, and the like.

These outcomes are as common as they are regrettable. Regrettable because it ought to be possible to develop an approach to justified and rational belief that comfortably places them within a general theory of rationality, thus connecting them not only with the concept of rational actions, plans, and strategies but also with our everyday assessments of each other's opinions.

A first step toward such an approach is to conceive rationality as goal oriented. Whether the question concerns the rationality of an action, belief, decision, intention, plan, or strategy, what is at issue is the effective pursuit of goals.

Success is not a prerequisite, however. What is rational can turn out badly. After all, some situations are such that no one could have been reasonably expected to foresee that what appeared to be the best option would lead to unwelcome consequences.

Considerations such as these suggest a template for rationality: an action A (decision, plan, intention, strategy, belief, etc.) is rational for an individual S if it is rational for S to believe that A would acceptably satisfy her goals.

An obvious drawback of this formulation is that it makes reference to rational belief, thus leaving us within the circle of notions we wish to understand. I will return to this issue in a moment, but note first that different kinds of goals can be taken into account in assessing the rationality of an action, decision, plan, or whatever. If it is rational for S to believe that doing A would effectively promote her economic goals, then A is rational for her in an economic sense. On the other hand, not all goals are economic. Some are self-interested but not economic (for example, ones concerning power, prestige, and the like), while still others are not self-interested at all (for example, ones concerning the welfare of family and friends). But then, even if A is rational for S in an economic sense, it need not be rational for her in a more general self-interested sense nor rational for her all things considered, since it might not be rational for her to believe that A would do an acceptably good job in promoting the full range of her goals, noneconomic as well as economic and non-self-interested as well as self-interested.

These observations point to a refinement of the template: an action A (decision, plan, intention, strategy, etc.) is rational in sense X for S if it is rational for S to believe that A will do an acceptably good job of satisfying her goals of type X.

Being clear about what goals and hence what kind of rationality are at issue is of particular importance for epistemology, because although there is nothing in principle wrong with evaluating beliefs in terms of how well they promote a variety of goals, epistemologists have traditionally been interested in a specific kind of rational belief, one that corresponds to the goal of now having beliefs that are accurate and comprehensive.

To understand the significance of the qualifier "now," imagine that S's prospects for having accurate and comprehensive beliefs in a year's time would be enhanced by believing something P for which she now lacks adequate evidence. For example, let P be a more favorable assessment of her intellectual talents than her evidence warrants, but suppose it is clear to her that if she were to believe P, she would become intellectually more confident, which would make her a more dedicated inquirer, which in turn would enhance her long-term prospects of having an accurate and comprehensive belief system. Despite these long-term intellectual benefits, there is an important sense of rational belief, indeed the very sense that traditionally has been of the most interest to epistemologists, in which it is not rational for her to believe P. A way of marking this distinction is to say that it is not epistemically rational for her to believe P, where this epistemic sense is understood in terms of the goal of now having accurate and comprehensive beliefs.

This goal has two aspects: comprehensiveness and accuracy. If the goal were only accuracy, the right strategy would be to believe very little (only that which is utterly certain, for example), whereas if the goal were only comprehensiveness, the right strategy would be to believe a great deal (whatever is more probable than not, for example). As the goal is stated, however, it is necessary to balance the risks of believing falsehoods against the benefits of believing truths.

There are delicate questions about how best to achieve this balance,[1] but it is not necessary to dwell on these questions, since the point of immediate relevance is that epistemologists have traditionally occupied themselves with this particular type of rational belief. Nor is it necessary to choose among competing accounts. Although foundationalists, coherentists, and others have different views about how best to explicate epistemically rational belief, what matters for purposes here is something they all have in common.

Namely, they all try to explicate the concept of epistemically rational belief without reference to any other concept of rationality. Foundationalists, for instance, understand epistemic rationality in terms of basic beliefs and a set of deductive and probabilistic relations by which other beliefs are supported by those that are basic. Moreover, they would view it as a defect if they had to make use of some notion of rationality (or a related notion, such as reasonability) in characterizing basicality or these support relations. Coherentists, on the other hand, explicate epistemic rationality in terms of a set of deductive and probabilistic relations among beliefs and such properties as simplicity and conservativeness, but they too would regard it as a flaw if their explication smuggled in a reference to a concept of rationality or a related concept. The same is true of other accounts of epistemically rational beliefs.

This point is of fundamental importance for the general theory of rationality because it provides the theory with an escape route from circularity. In particular, the template of rationality can be expressed using the concept of epistemically rational belief: an action A (decision, plan, intention, etc.) is rational in sense X for S just in case it is epistemically rational for S to believe that A will do an acceptably good job of satisfying goals of kind X.

Because the concept of epistemically rational belief is explicated without making use of any other notion of rationality or a close cognate, the template is now theoretically respectable. It makes no noneliminable reference to a concept of rationality. Epistemically rational belief functions as a theoretical anchor for other concepts of rationality.[2]

In this template, "X" can refer to all of S's goals or only a subset of them. There is, accordingly, a risk of confusion if one does not specify the kind of goal and hence the kind of rationality at issue in assessing an action, decision, plan, or strategy. The same possibilities for confusion arise when the issue is the rationality of beliefs. Although, as mentioned above, epistemologists have traditionally been interested in assessing beliefs in terms of the specific intellectual goal of now having accurate and comprehensive beliefs, the template implies that in principle there is nothing wrong with assessing beliefs in terms of how well they promote other goals, including the total constellation of S's goals (practical as well as intellectual, and long term as well as immediate).

In everyday contexts, however, we rarely do so, at least not explicitly. The question is, why not? The two observations made in chapter 10 provide the answer. First, in deliberations about what to believe about a claim, it is usually ineffectual to cite considerations that do not purport to be related to its truth, since they are not the kind of reasons that consciously persuade us to believe. Second, it is ordinarily redundant to focus on non-truth-related reasons for belief, because what it is rational for us to believe when all of our goals are taken into account is usually identical with what it is epistemically rational for us to believe. This is so because in all but a few unusual situations, the beliefs that are likely to do the best overall job of promoting the total constellation of our goals are those that are comprehensive and accurate, since only by having such beliefs are we likely to be able to fashion effective strategies for achieving our goals.

Although practical considerations typically do not consciously and directly enter into our everyday assessments of each other's beliefs or into our own deliberations about what to believe, they do, as was also pointed out in chapter 10, deeply influence what it is rational for us to believe. They do so by determining the direction and extent of our inquiries. None of us are purely intellectual beings. We all have a wide variety of ends, and these ends determine which inquiries it is reasonable to undertake and how much time and energy to devote to them.

Our everyday assessments of each other's beliefs take into account this reality by being "reason saturated." They are concerned, for example, with whether someone has been reasonably thorough in gathering evidence and then reasonably careful in deliberating about it, where the standards of reasonability at work here are realistic ones. They reflect the fact that we all have nonintellectual interests, goals, and needs, which constrain the amount of time and effort it is appropriate to devote to investigating an issue. Only a concept that is sensitive to these questions of resource allocation is capable of capturing the spirit of these everyday evaluations.

Justified belief, I maintain, is just such a concept, but as I understand it, the concept is closely associated with responsible believing as opposed to what is required to turn true belief into knowledge. In particular, making use of the general template of rationality, S justifiably believes P if it is epistemically rational for her to believe that her procedures with respect to P have been acceptable given all her goals and given also the limitations on her time and capacities.

Justified belief, so understood, is able to do justice to the fact that there are many matters about which it is not especially important to have accurate and comprehensive beliefs, and hence it is not appropriate to spend much time and effort gathering information and thinking about them. The core intuition here is that having justified beliefs requires one to be a responsible believer, but being responsible does not necessarily require one to go to extraordinary lengths in trying to discover the truth about an issue. More exactly, it does not require this unless the issue itself is extraordinarily important, in which case extraordinary diligence is precisely what is called for.

The standards of justified belief thus vary with the importance of the issue, with high importance translating into demanding standards and low importance into less demanding ones. In other words, just what one would expect.[3]

Chapter 27

The Core Concepts of Epistemology

With the concepts of epistemically rational and justified belief situated within a philosophically respectable and perfectly general theory of rationality, and with knowledge understood as true belief plus adequate information, epistemology is reoriented.

The core concepts of the reoriented epistemology are true belief and epistemically rational belief. Knowledge and justified belief are derivative concepts[1] explicated in terms of these core concepts together with human goals, needs, and values, which explains why the standards of both knowledge and justified belief become more demanding as the stakes go up. In the case of knowledge there cannot be important truths of which one is unaware, and in the case of justified belief the level of effort one expends in gathering evidence and deliberating should be commensurate with what it is epistemically rational to believe about the importance of the matter at hand.

The structure of epistemology can thus be represented by two conceptual chains. In Chain 1, the concept of epistemically rational belief in conjunction with considerations about the importance of the issue in question generates the concept of justified belief. In Chain 2, the concept of true belief in conjunction with considerations about the importance of truths one is aware of and not aware of generates the concept of knowledge.

Chain 1 is located within a general theory of rationality, at the heart of which is a template: an action A (decision, plan, strategy, or whatever) is rational in sense X for S if it is epistemically rational for S to believe that A will do an acceptably good job of satisfying her goals of type X. The template is perfectly general in the sense that it can be used to distinguish different kinds of rationality (economic rationality, rationality all things considered, epistemic rationality, etc.) and can also be used to understand the rationality of different kinds of phenomena (actions, decisions, plans, strategies, beliefs, etc.).

Chain 2 has been the primary focus of this book, the major thesis of which is that knowledge is a matter of having adequate information, where the test of adequacy is there being no important truths that one lacks.

There are no necessary links between the two chains, only contingent ones. This is so despite the fact that the defining goal of epistemically rational belief is that of now having true and comprehensive beliefs. So, when all goes well, epistemically rational beliefs are good candidates for knowledge.

Similarly for justified beliefs. Although practical considerations have an important role in determining what one justifiably believes, they do so by affecting the direction and extent of inquiry, after which they ordinarily drop out as irrelevant, with the aim then being to have true beliefs and avoid false ones. So once again, when things work out well, beliefs that are justified are plausible candidates for knowledge.

Things need not always work out, however. Beliefs can be epistemically rational and yet be mistaken, and so too can justified beliefs. They can even be thoroughly mistaken, as brain-in-the-vat and other such skeptical scenarios illustrate.

Nor is there a necessary link between knowledge and epistemic rationality or justification from the opposite direction. Neither epistemic rationality nor justification need enter into the explanation of when and how a true belief rises to the level of knowledge. To explain why S's belief is an instance of knowledge, it is sufficient to note that it is true and she believes enough surrounding truths so that there is no important gap in her information. Nothing more is required.

To be sure, when S knows P, it is usually the case that she and her belief have various other merits. Her belief may be justified; it may have been reliably produced; it may track the truth in close counterfactual situations; S herself may have been meticulous in gathering evidence about P; she may have been appropriately careful and thorough in deliberating about this evidence; and she may possess various intellectual virtues that played a role in her coming to believe P. These merits are not required to explain why she knows P, however. Except in a few rare and strange situations in which knowledge is blocked, S knows P if she believes P, P is true, and there are no important truths she lacks.

Notes

Chapter 1. An Observation

1. I am thus setting aside suggestions to the effect that the concepts of belief or truth be abandoned. See Paul Boghossian's critique of the view that there are no truths, only truths relative to a particular way of thinking, in *Fear of Knowledge* (Oxford: Oxford University Press, 2006), chaps. 3 and 4. See my *Working Without a Net* (Oxford: Oxford University Press, 1993), chap. 4, for an argument against the idea that the concept of belief should be discarded in favor of a concept of degrees of belief.

Chapter 2. Post-Gettier Accounts of Knowledge

1. Edmund Gettier, "Is Justified True Belief Knowledge?" *Analysis* 25 (1963): 121–23.

2. Roderick Chisholm, *Theory of Knowledge*, 2nd ed. (Englewood Cliffs, NJ: Prentice-Hall, 1977), 102–18; Ernest Sosa, "Epistemic Presupposition," in *Justification and Knowledge*, ed. George S. Pappas (Dordrecht: Reidel, 1979), 79–92; and Ernest Sosa, "How Do You Know?" in *Knowledge in Perspective*, ed. Ernest Sosa (Cambridge: Cambridge University Press, 1991), 19–34.

3. Robert Audi, *The Structure of Justification* (Cambridge: Cambridge University Press, 1993); Peter Klein, *Certainty: A Refutation of Scepticism* (Minneapolis: University of Minnesota Press, 1981); Keith Lehrer, *Knowledge* (Oxford: Oxford University Press, 1974); John Pollock, *Contemporary Theories of Knowledge* (Totowa, NJ: Rowman and

Littlefield, 1986); and Marshall Swain, *Reasons and Knowledge* (Ithaca, NY: Cornell University Press, 1981).

4. Alvin Goldman, *Epistemology and Cognition* (Cambridge, MA: Harvard University Press, 1986).

5. Robert Nozick, *Philosophical Explanations* (Cambridge, MA: Harvard University Press, 1981).

6. Alvin Plantinga, *Warrant: The Current Debate* (Oxford: Oxford University Press, 1993).

7. For example, see D. M. Armstrong, *Belief, Truth, and Knowledge* (Cambridge: Cambridge University Press, 1973); Fred Dretske, *Knowledge and the Flow of Information* (Cambridge, MA: MIT Press, 1981); David Lewis, "Elusive Knowledge," *Australasian Journal of Philosophy* 74 (1996): 549–67; and Ernest Sosa, *Knowledge in Perspective*, esp. chaps. 13–16.

CHAPTER 3. KNOWLEDGE STORIES

1. See Alvin Goldman, "Discrimination and Perceptual Knowledge," *Journal of Philosophy* 73 (1976): 771–91; and Carl Ginet, "The Fourth Condition," in *Philosophical Analysis: A Defense by Example*, ed. David F. Austin (Dordrecht: Kluwer, 1988).

CHAPTER 4. INTUITIONS ABOUT KNOWLEDGE

1. Noam Chomsky, *Rules and Representation* (New York: Columbia University Press, 1980), 82.

2. David Lewis, "Scorekeeping in a Language Game," in *Philosophical Papers*, vol. 1 (New York: Oxford University Press, 1983).

3. See, for example, Peter Unger, *Ignorance: A Case for Scepticism* (Oxford: Oxford University Press, 1975 and 2002); Richard Fumerton, *Epistemology* (Oxford: Blackwell, 2006), esp. chap. 2; and Richard Fumerton, *Meta-epistemology and Skepticism* (Boston: Rowan and Littlefield, 1996).

4. See chap. 24 for a discussion of collective knowledge and its relation to individual knowledge.

5. Here is another such story. When asked to provide the decimal expansion of pi to five decimal places, *S* immediately responds, "3.14159." *S* understands that pi is the ratio of a circle's circumference to its diameter, but she is otherwise largely ignorant of its properties (that pi is an irrational number, etc.) and its uses in geometry (that pi can be used to calculate the area of a circle via the formula $A = \pi r2$,

etc.). Nevertheless, it seems as if she at least knows this much about pi: that its decimal expansion to five decimal places is 3.14159. For other such cases, see John Hawthorne, *Knowledge and Lotteries* (Oxford: Oxford University Press, 2004), 68–69; Crispin Sartwell, "Why Knowledge is Merely True Belief," *Journal of Philosophy* 89 (1992): 167–80; and Sartwell, "Knowledge as Merely True Belief," *American Philosophical Quarterly* 28 (1991): 157–64).

6. There are other ways of making George's ignorance of the facades at other locations look less significant. Suppose after gazing out the window for a moment, he gets out of his car, walks up to and around the barn, and observes it from all sides. In this telling of the story, he has more detailed information about this specific location, and it is this that makes his ignorance of the facades at other locations seem less important.

7. This is a point that coherence theorists emphasize in order to explain how their theory is compatible with simple observational and memory beliefs being justified. See, for example, Gilbert Harman, *Change in View* (Cambridge, MA: MIT Press, 1986); and Keith Lehrer, *Knowledge* (Oxford: Oxford University Press, 1974).

8. As the Marathon story illustrates, one way of narrowing the focus is to have the story revolve around a specific question and then to imagine circumstances in which it is important for the subject to know how to answer that question. Knowing how is towing knowing that behind it in its wake.

CHAPTER 5. IMPORTANT TRUTHS

1. More cautiously, their apparent disagreement. "Apparent" because contextualists maintain that knowledge claims are contextually dependent, and as a result it is possible for one person to assert that *S* knows *P* and another to assert that she does not know *P* and for both to be correct. For discussions of contextualism and related issues, see Stewart Cohen, "Contextualist Solutions to Epistemological Problems: Skepticism, Gettier, and the Lottery," *Australasian Journal of Philosophy* 76 (1998): 289–306; Cohen, "Contextualism Defended," *Philosophical Studies* 103 (2001): 87–98; Keith DeRose, "Contextualism and Knowledge Attributions," *Philosophy and Phenomenological Research* 52 (1992): 913–29; Richard Feldman, "Skeptical Problems, Contextualist Solutions," *Philosophical Studies* 103 (2001): 61–85; Hawthorne, *Knowledge and Lotteries*; David Lewis, "Elusive Knowledge," *Australasian Journal of Philosophy* 74 (1996): 549–67; James Pryor, "Highlights of Recent Epistemology," *British Journal for the Philosophy of Science* 52

(2001): 95–124; and Peter Unger, "The Cone Model of Knowledge," *Philosophical Topics* 14 (1986): 125–78.

2. This is all the more likely if the two stories are not told together. If told separately, the story about the toaster may strike listeners as a case of knowledge for the reasons cited above, but when told alongside the story about the air purification equipment (in the same performance, as it were), the intuitions invoked by the latter tend to get transferred to it, so that the gap in the foreman's information about the malfunction in the toaster's warning light seems more important. In effect, the reaction of listeners may now be, "The gap is significant because look at the implications of a similar kind of gap in the chemical plant case." This is another example of how the context of presentation can influence the reactions that a knowledge story elicits.

3. Jason Stanley, *Knowledge and Practical Interests* (Oxford: Oxford University Press, 2005). See also Jeremy Fantl and Matthew Mc-Grath, "Evidence, Pragmatics, and Justification," *Philosophical Review* 111 (2002): 67–94; and Hawthorne, *Knowledge and Lotteries*, chap. 4.

4. Brian McLaughlin first suggested to me that closeness be thought of as a component of importance.

5. For some other examples of narrow knowledge, see the discussions of introspective, perceptual, and testimonial knowledge in chaps. 21 and 22.

6. Where does this leave the dispute over whether knowledge claims are contextually dependent? Questions of contextualism on this approach hinge on whether there is a plausible noncontextualist treatment of adequate information. As the above discussion shows, there are challenges in providing such a treatment, but nothing in the approach per se precludes this.

CHAPTER 6. MAXIMALLY ACCURATE AND COMPREHENSIVE BELIEFS

1. A passage from the *Aeneid*, trans. Allen Mandelbaum, bk. 3, lines 576–91 (New York: Bantam, 1971), describing the cavern of the prophet Sibyl makes this point in a splendidly imaginative way:

When on your way you reach the town of Cumae,
the sacred lakes, the loud wood of Avernus,
there you will see the frenzied prophetess.
Deep in her cave of rock she charts the fates,
Consigning to the leaves her words and symbols.
Whatever verses she has written down
Upon the leaves, she puts them in place and order

And then abandons them inside her cavern.
When all is still, that order is not troubled;
But when soft winds are stirring and the door,
Turning upon its hinge, disturbs the tender
Leaves, then she never cares to catch the verses
That flutter through the hollow grotto, never
Recalls their place and joins them all together.
Her visitors, when they have had no counsel,
Depart, and then detest the Sibyl's cavern.

2. See the related discussion in chap. 18.

3. See, for example, Goldman, *Epistemology and Cognition*, 106–9.

4. See Donald Davidson, "On the Very Idea of a Conceptual Scheme," *Proceedings and Addresses of the American Philosophical Association* 17 (1973–1974): 5–20; and Davidson, "A Coherence Theory of Truth and Knowledge," in *The Philosophy of Donald Davidson: Perspectives on Truth and Interpretation*, ed. Ernest LePore (London: Basil Blackwell, 1986), 307–19.

5. Or the point might be approached from the opposite direction, namely, a world in which Sally's beliefs do not meet minimum standards of coherence despite being maximally accurate and comprehensive is not a world in which knowledge is possible; it is too chaotic for Sally or anyone else to have knowledge of it. See the related discussion in chap. 7.

CHAPTER 7. THE BEETLE IN THE BOX

1. John Hawthorne first pointed out to me the relevance of this kind of case.

2. James Pryor first suggested to me the idea of formulating the point here in terms of conditions that interfere with the basic conditions of knowledge.

CHAPTER 8. KNOWLEDGE BLOCKS

1. "Significant information" because as with any situation, there is no end to the number of truths associated with there being a beetle in the box. Since there is a beetle in the box, it is also true that there is either a beetle or a coin in the box; since the star Antares is larger than the star Spica, it is also true that (there is a beetle in the box and Antares is larger than Spica); and so on. As noted in chap. 6, however, not just any large collection of truths puts one in a position to know.

2. I owe this case to Paul Boghossian.

3. See related discussion in chap. 13.

CHAPTER 9. THE THEORY OF KNOWLEDGE AND THEORY OF JUSTIFIED BELIEF

1. Gettier, "Is Justified True Belief Knowledge?"

2. Chap. 26 sketches a theory of justified belief with a focus on responsible believing.

3. There are others who have repudiated the Gettier game. See, for example, Timothy Williamson, *Knowledge and Its Limits* (Oxford: Oxford University Press, 2000). Williamson's "knowledge first" approach rejects the assumption that justified belief is an ingredient of knowledge. It instead makes knowledge into an ingredient of justified belief, the core assumptions being that one is justified in believing only that which is supported by one's evidence and that one's evidence is limited to what one knows. On this view, knowledge and justified belief are still conceptually married, only in the reverse direction, but once again, this is a forced marriage producing awkward results. For details, see Richard Foley, "Review of Timothy Williamson, *Knowledge and Its Limits*," *Mind* 111 (2002): 726–30.

CHAPTER 10. THE VALUE OF TRUE BELIEF

1. Bernard Williams, "Deciding to Believe," in *Problems of the Self* (New York: Cambridge University Press, 1973); and John Searle, *Intentionality* (New York: Cambridge University Press, 1983), 8. See related views in Paul Boghossian, "The Normativity of Content," *Philosophical Issues* 13 (2003): 31–45: David Velleman, *The Possibility of Practical Reason* (Oxford: Oxford University Press, 2000), 16; Nishi Shaw, "How Truth Governs Belief," *Philosophical Review* 112 (2003): 447–83; and Michael Lynch, *True to Life* (Cambridge, MA: MIT Press, 2004).

CHAPTER 11. THE VALUE OF KNOWLEDGE

1. See Marian David, "Truth as the Epistemic Goal, in *Knowledge, Truth, and Duty*, ed. Matthias Steup (Oxford: Oxford University Press, 2001); Michael DePaul, "Value Monism in Epistemology," in Steup,

Knowledge, Truth; Ward Jones, "Why Do We Value Knowledge?" *American Philosophical Quarterly* 34 (1997): 423–39; Jonathan Kvanvig, "Why Should Inquiring Minds Want to Know? *Meno* Problems and Epistemological Axiology," *Monist* 81 (1998): 426–51; Jonathan Kvanvig, *The Value of Knowledge and the Pursuit of Understanding* (Cambridge: Cambridge University Press, 2003); Stephen Maitzen, "Our Errant Epistemic Aim," *Philosophy and Phenomenological Research* 55 (1995): 869–76; Crispin Sartwell, "Why Knowledge Is Merely True Belief," *Journal of Philosophy* 88 (1992): 167–80; and Sartwell "Knowledge as Merely True Belief," *American Philosophical Quarterly* 28 (1991): 157–64.

2. An exception, of course, is when *P* is a proposition about oneself.

3. Compare with Ward Jones, "The Goods and Motivation of Believing," in *The Value of Knowledge*, ed. Adrian Haddock, Alan Millar, and Duncan Pritchard (Oxford: Oxford University Press, 2008), 139–62.

4. Compare with Linda Zagzebski, "The Search for the Source of the Epistemic Good," *Metaphilosophy* 34 (2003): 12–28.

5. See Haddock, Millar, and Pritchard, *Value of Knowledge*, for a discussion of some of these responses.

6. Compare with Ralph Wedgwood: "[T]he only acceptable explanation of why we should aim at knowledge must be grounded in the more fundamental principle that we should aim at getting to the truth." Wedgwood, "The Aim of Belief," *Philosophical Perspectives* 16 (2002): 267–97.

7. Wayne Riggs first suggested to me the usefulness of this way of framing the issue.

8. A sampling of other views on the value of knowledge (in addition to those cited earlier) includes Edward Craig, *Knowledge and the State of Nature* (Oxford: Oxford University Press, 1990); John Greco, "Knowledge as Credit for True Belief," in *Intellectual Virtue: Perspectives from Ethics and Epistemology*, ed. Michael DePaul and Linda Zagzebski (Oxford: Oxford University Press, 2003); Hawthorne, *Knowledge and Lotteries*; Wayne D. Riggs, "Reliability and the Value of Knowledge," *Philosophy and Phenomenological Research* 64 (2002): 79–96; Ernest Sosa, "The Love of Truth," in *Virtue Epistemology: Essays on Epistemic Virtue and Responsibility*, ed. Abrol Fairweather and Linda Zagzebski (Oxford: Oxford University Press, 2000); and Linda Zagzebski, *Virtues of the Mind: An Inquiry into the Nature of Virtue and the Ethical Foundations of Knowledge* (Cambridge: Cambridge University Press, 1996).

CHAPTER 13. REVERSE LOTTERY STORIES

1. Fred Dretske first pointed out to me the significance of these stories.

2. Barry Loewer first pointed out this issue to me.

3. See chap. 6.

CHAPTER 14. LUCKY KNOWLEDGE

1. I owe this case to David Christensen.

2. Contrast with Ernest Sosa, "How to Defeat Opposition to Moore," in *Philosophical Perspectives* 13 (2000): 141–54; and Williamson, *Knowledge and Its Limits*. The assumption that knowledge cannot arise from luck leads Sosa and Williamson, among others, to propose a safety condition on knowledge, according to which one knows *P* only if one's true belief *P* could not easily have been false. For other views linking knowledge to the absence of luck, see Greco, "Knowledge as Credit for True Belief"; and Zagzebski, *Virtues of the Mind*.

CHAPTER 15. CLOSURE AND SKEPTICISM

1. For a general discussion of epistemic closure, see Hawthorne, *Knowledge and Lotteries*.

2. See esp. Fumerton, *Epistemology*, 12–32; Unger, *Ignorance: A Case for Scepticism*; and David Lewis, "Elusive Knowledge," in *Papers in Metaphysics and Epistemology* (Cambridge: Cambridge University Press, 1999), 418–45.

3. See the related discussion in chap. 26, and also Foley, *Working Without a Net*, esp. chap. 2.

CHAPTER 16. DISJUNCTIONS

1. I owe Ernest Sosa and Hartry Field for raising this issue.

2. Here is an analogous case from Ernest Sosa: *S* comes into a room filled with people and hears someone yell a threat; *S* can have enough information to know that someone in the room threatened her without being aware which person has done so.

CHAPTER 18. INSTABILITY AND KNOWLEDGE

1. I owe this case to Alvin Plantinga.

2. Another out of the ordinary element of the story here is the degree of external control over Sally's states. It is a demon who alternatively causes Sally for two seconds to have beliefs as accurate and comprehensive as humanly possible and then for two seconds beliefs that are massively mistaken. Just as we may be reluctant to grant the status of belief to states that flip on and off at two-second intervals, so too we may think that only states with a minimal degree of freedom from direct external control qualify as genuine beliefs.

CHAPTER 19. MISLEADING DEFEATERS

1. See chap. 9.

2. Peter Klein, *Certainty* (Minneapolis: University of Minnesota Press, 1981).

3. Again, see Klein, *Certainty*; also Klein, "Misleading Evidence and the Restoration of Justification," *Philosophical Studies* 37 (1980): 81–89.

CHAPTER 20. BELIEVING THAT I DON'T KNOW

1. Assertions of the form "I believe *P* but do not know *P*" are thus to be contrasted with those of the form "I believe *P* but *P* is not true." The former are both common and easy to understand, while the latter can seem paradoxical. There is no logical inconsistency involved in asserting the latter (it is not impossible for me to believe *P* and for *P* not to be true), but there is a pragmatic inconsistency. When I assert the second half of the sentence ("*P* is not true"), listeners are normally entitled to infer that I believe not-*P*, but this is at odds with what I am asserting in the first half of the sentence.

2. One possible explanation is that knowledge requires a high degree of confidence in the proposition's truth, but in cases in which I am willing to admit that I believe but don't know *P*, my degree of confidence in *P* falls below what is required for knowledge. Not all such cases can be accounted for in this manner, however. In a lottery, my degree of confidence that my ticket will not win can asymptotically approach 1.0 as the number of tickets in the lottery increases, and yet I may still believe that I don't know that it will not win.

CHAPTER 21. INTROSPECTIVE KNOWLEDGE

1. See Ludwig Wittgenstein, *Philosophical Investigations* (London: Blackwell, 1974), § 246; II. xi (222).

2. See Tyler Burge on the infallibility of such beliefs, "Individualism and Self-Knowledge," *Journal of Philosophy* 85 (1988): 649–62.

3. See Crispin Wright on positive presumptiveness, "Wittgenstein's Later Philosophy of Mind: Sensation, Privacy, and Intention," *Journal of Philosophy* 86 (1989): 622–34.

4. Williamson, *Knowledge and Its Limits*); Roderick Chisholm, *Theory of Knowledge*, 3rd ed. (Englewood Cliffs, NJ: Prentice-Hall), 1989.

5. Here is a related issue. Suppose at the current time t S has a true belief that at time $t + n$ she will have a headache. Regardless of how much information she has at t, she will be in an even better position at $t + n$ to know whether at that moment she has a headache. But isn't this puzzling? After all, although she will at $t + n$ have a true belief that she then has a headache, at the current time t she already has a true belief to this effect. The explanation, however, is that her current belief does not have the same content as the belief she will have at $t + n$, since it does not (and cannot) involve a special awareness of the characteristic unpleasantness of the headache. Thus, at time $t + n$ she will have information about her headache that she cannot possibly now have (and that others also cannot possibly have). I owe Evan Williams and Tim Maudlin for raising this issue.

CHAPTER 22. PERCEPTUAL KNOWLEDGE

1. See chap. 5.

2. See the discussion in chap. 4.

CHAPTER 23. A PRIORI KNOWLEDGE

1. See, for example, Jason Stanley and Timothy Williamson, "Knowing How," *Journal of Philosophy* 98 (2001): 411–44.

2. A related point is that understanding simple concepts involves understanding how to make relevant inferences involving them. Understanding the concept of red, for example, brings with it the understanding that if something is red, it is colored. If one doesn't know how to make the most obvious and immediate inferences involving the concept of red, one doesn't really understand the concept and

hence cannot have beliefs involving it. See Paul Boghossian, "How Are Objective Epistemic Reasons Possible?" *Philosophical Studies* 106 (December 2001): 340–80.

CHAPTER 24. COLLECTIVE KNOWLEDGE

1. Note, however, that when nonexperts defer to experts, sometimes what they come to believe is that a particular sentence is true as opposed to the proposition expressed by the sentence. A nonexpert may accept that the sentence "Bosons but not fermions can occupy the same quantum state" is true because she has heard particle physicists endorse it, but if the nonexpert lacks the relevant training in physics, she will not be able to grasp, and hence will not believe, the proposition expressed by this sentence.

2. "The method of modern science is social in respect to the solidarity of its efforts. The scientific world is like a colony of insects in that the individual strives to produce that which he cannot himself hope to enjoy. One generation collects premises in order that a distant generation may discover what they mean. When a problem comes before the scientific world, a hundred men immediately set their energies to work on it. One contributes this, another that. Another company, standing on the shoulders of the first, strikes a little higher until at last the parapet is attained." *Collected Papers of Charles Sanders Peirce*, ed., Charles Hartshorne, Paul Weiss, and Arthur W. Burks (Cambridge, MA: Harvard University Press, 1931–1958), 7.87.

3. C. P. Snow, *The Two Cultures* (Cambridge: Cambridge University Press, 1993).

CHAPTER 25. A LOOK BACK

1. Richard Foley, *Working Without a Net* (Oxford: Oxford University Press, 1993).

CHAPTER 26. EPISTEMOLOGY WITHIN A GENERAL THEORY OF RATIONALITY

1. One such question concerns whether it can be epistemically rational for an individual to believe propositions that she realizes are jointly inconsistent and hence cannot possibly all be true. It is some-

times assumed that the answer must be no, but notice that in many contexts it is rational to pursue a strategy that one knows in advance cannot possibly result in an ideal outcome. Think of betting and investment contexts in which it is often rational to prefer a moderate but necessarily flawed strategy to a possibly flawless but more risky one. Compare with the discussion of the lottery and preface in chap. 12. See also my *Working Without a Net*, esp. chap. 4.

2. The concept of epistemically rational belief is itself an instantiation of this template. Inserting the epistemic goal into the template for "goals of type X" results in the following: believing P is rational in an epistemic sense if it is epistemically rational for S to believe that believing P would acceptably satisfy the epistemic goal of S's now having accurate and comprehensive beliefs. This instantiation is tautological, which for the sake of generality of the template is just what is called for.

3. For more details on this way of understanding justified belief, see Richard Foley, "An Epistemology that Matters," in *Essays in Honor of Philip Quinn*, ed. Paul J. Weithman; and Richard Foley, "The Foundational Role of Epistemology in a General Theory of Rationality," in Zagzebski and Fairweather, *Virtue Epistemology*.

CHAPTER 27. THE CORE CONCEPTS OF EPISTEMOLOGY

1. See Fumerton, *Epistemology*, chap. 2; and Mark Kaplan, "It's What You Know that Counts," *Journal of Philosophy* 82 (1985): 350–63, each of whom takes a different route to the same conclusion that knowledge is a secondary epistemic concept. For an opposing view, see Williamson, *Knowledge and Its Limits*.

Index